ACCESSING HIGHER TRUTH

MELINDA H. CONNOR

D.D. Ph.D. AMP FAM

Other books by Melinda H. Connor

Ten daily needs

See auras

Accessing Higher Truth

Resonance Modulation: Biofield Basics

Advanced Body Reading

Casetaking for the Energy Practitioner

Professional Practice for the Energy Healing Practitioner

ACCESSING HIGHER TRUTH

MELINDA H. CONNOR
D.D. Ph.D. AMP FAM

The material contained in this book has been written for informational purposes and is not intended as a substitute for medical advice, nor is it intended to diagnose, treat, cure, or prevent disease. If you have a medical issue or illness, consult a qualified physician.

Published by

ARNICA PRESS
www.ArnicaPress.com

Copyright © 2016, 2025 Melinda H. Connor

Written by Melinda H. Connor

Cover Photo: Shutterstock

Manufactured in the United States of America

ISBN: 978-1-955354-78-3

All rights reserved. No part of this book may be reproduced or transmitted in any form or by any means, electronic or mechanical, including photocopying, recording, or by any information storage and retrieval system, without the prior written permission from the Author. This book may not be AI scraped or utilized in AI processes unless permission in writing is received by the author.

THE DISCLAIMER
PLEASE READ BEFORE READING THE BOOK

The information contained in this book, including ideas, suggestions, exercises, meditations, and other materials, is provided only as general information and is solely intended for your own self-improvement and is not meant to be a substitute for medical or psychological treatment and does not replace the services of health care professionals. If you experience any emotional distress or physical discomfort using any ideas, suggestions, exercises, or meditations contained in this book, you are advised to stop and to seek professional care, if appropriate.

Publishing of the information contained in this book is not intended to create a client-therapist or any other type of professional relationship between the reader and the author. The author does not make any warranty, guarantee, or prediction regarding the outcome of an individual using this book for any particular purpose or issue.

You agree to assume and accept full responsibility for any and all risks associated with using any of the ideas, suggestions, exercises, or meditations, described in this book and agree to accept full and complete responsibility for applying what you may learn from reading this book.

By continuing to read this book you agree to fully release, indemnify, and hold harmless, the author, and others associated with the publication of this book from any claim or liability and for any damage or injury of whatsoever kind or nature which you may incur arising at any time out of or in relation to your use of the information presented in this book. If any court of law rules that any part of the Disclaimer is invalid, the Disclaimer stands as if those parts were struck out.

**BY CONTINUING TO READ THE BOOK
YOU AGREE TO THE DISCLAIMER**

PLEASE ENJOY THE BOOK AND HAVE FUN!

To Drs. Gary Schwartz and Iris Bell,

Thank you for the mentoring and the wisdom.
I could not have developed this far without your training,
your mentoring and your many kindnesses over the years.
I am profoundly and deeply grateful to you both.
I am only now beginning to really comprehend
how good the training is that you gave me
in the process of learning to be an academic,
a teacher and a scientist.

Blessings,

Melinda

ACKNOWLEDGMENTS

Deep gratitude to and a thank you for your kindness and your support and for acting as my readers:

Dr. Douglas Schneider, Jeremy Sharpe MBA, Rev. Tiffany Barsotti, Rev. Tracy Parker, Atty Harvey S. Bass, Caitlin Connor (abd)DAOM, Shelagh Smith, Chiara Marrapodi, and Dr. Ann Nunley. To the team at Holos University Graduate Seminary, you are amazing and I am grateful.

Special thanks go once again to Dr. Kendra H. Gaines for her editorial skills. I am deeply grateful for your wisdom. Any errors are mine alone.

To everyone else who had a hand in this book:
Thank You, Thank You, Thank You!!!

TABLE OF CONTENTS

Disclaimer 5
Acknowledgments 9
Introduction 17

CHAPTER ONE ~ What is emotion? 19
Definition of emotion 20
How are your emotions experienced? 20
Defensive patterns 21
Emotional response is faster than thought 23
Healing through emotional expression 24
Grounding as the start 25
Draining excess emotion 29
Centering and aligning 32
Let the heart open 33

CHAPTER TWO ~ What is intuition? 35
Definition of intuition 35
Where does intuitive information come from? 35
How does intuition present itself? 36
    Memory 37
    Sound bytes 38
    Smells 39
    Tastes 40
    Floating images 41

The Flash 42
The Aha moment 43
River of information 44
A complete form 45
Moments of disorientation or disconnection 46
Listening to the quiet inner voice............................47
Allowing yourself to act on what you hear
when the internal voice is quiet...............................48
Noticing your disregard..48
Noticing not wanting to hear...................................49
Healing through intuition with wisdom..................51

CHAPTER THREE ~ What is compassion? 53
Definition of compassion...54
How does one create calm-passion?.........................54
Where does a spiritual connection fit? 55
The question of Karma and redemption 56
How to do forgiveness of self 58
How to forgive the other..59

CHAPTER FOUR ~ Basic Methods of Accessing Intuitive Information 61
Reaching up 62
Allowing return flow of information.......................62
Reaching into the heart..63
Searching the waters of the body 66
Surrendering to the divine.......................................67
Rolling forward or backward in time......................68
Connecting to core...69
Using the Minds Eye access.....................................70

CHAPTER FIVE ~ Interpretation of information ...73
The Ego self and the needs of the unconscious 74
What is your unconscious vocabulary? 76
Separation of the needs of the self from the need
to service the longing of the other..78
Are you stereo-typing or looking
at categories of behavior?..78
Are you sharing phony psychobabble? 80
Don't interpret! Say what you saw exactly 82

CHAPTER SIX ~ Appropriate Sharing of Intuitive Information 85
What to do when you get nothing..88
Support system assessment..88
Power and Control 89
    Over sharing..91
    Impact of the information.......................................92
    How to share/Weight of the words 92
    Do not reinforce negative information
    because the situation can change 93
    Do not get caught in parlor games 93
    Limits of the Intuitive..94
    Don't force your interpretation on someone else 94
    Do not decide anything for the Individual......................95
    Do not remove the Individuals
    opportunity for transformation 95

CHAPTER SEVEN ~ Inside and Outside the self ..97
Genetics and Epigenetics: Limits of transformation............97
Gained and lost opportunities...98
Fear as a choice 98
Fear of Being Noticed..99

Techniques of down regulation and forgiveness..................99
Choosing Joy and Happiness..100
Being different in a good way..100

CHAPTER EIGHT ~ Final Words 103
Final Words 103
Appendix A - Rules of Sharing...105

CHAPTER NINE ~ WORKBOOK 109
Introduction to Workbook 111
How to use the Workbook 111
Workbook for Chapter 1:
   What is emotion? 113
Workbook for Chapter 2:
   What is intuition? 131
Workbook for Chapter 3:
   What is compassion? 149
Workbook for Chapter 4:
   Basic Methods of Accessing Intuitive Information 157
Workbook for Chapter 5:
   Interpretation of information 173
Workbook for Chapter 6:
   Appropriate Sharing of Intuitive Information 179
Workbook for Chapter 7:
   Inside and Outside the self 187
Workbook for Chapter 8:
   Final Words 191
Appendix A: Rules of Sharing 193
Appendix B: Practice Sharing Information Exercises 195

About the Author..197

INTRODUCTION

The act of sharing intuitive information needs to be held as a sacred trust and in today's society it is not often held in that way. Words have weight. Words can help and can harm. I would both invite and caution those who are embarking on this process of accessing intuitive information to act with great discretion, wisdom, compassion and truth. Your actions have consequences. Your actions result in other actions. Individuals will make life choices based on the information which you share. Be strict with yourself to only share truth as you know it at the time. Do not interpret the information. Instead share exactly what you see and how you received the information. It is for the individual with whom you are sharing to make the interpretation of the information. Do not fall into the trap of telling people how to run their lives.

It is easy in today's world to want to be thought of as a powerful person. Instead of seeking this form, seek to become a person respected for their integrity, compassion and warmth. For it is through appreciating the person who has come to you for wisdom and insight and seeing their act as a sacred trust that you will become truly successful.

Remember joy. The act of sharing information is an act of creation. The world is a complex and often a difficult place. If by each act of sharing you create joy, you support the world becoming a better place. If with each act of sharing you can support a person in the process of creating wisdom for their life you help our world heal just that bit more. If with each act of sharing you support the teaching process and the development and the sharing of life skills, a person may then create a positive and beautiful life change again and again in their life.

Develop and learn to hold your center as you study this material and methodology. Dig deeply inside of the self to find pathways to truth which you will be able to hold with integrity no matter what happens in your own life. Be honorable, hold appropriate boundaries and find joy in every moment in your own life so that you may show with your life the truth of the information you bring to others.

Journey in Grace,

Melinda

CHAPTER ONE

WHAT IS EMOTION?

The best place to start this journey is with emotion. Emotion causes us to dance with joy and cry out with sorrow. It can be cleansing and/or it can be overwhelming. The power of our emotions is one of the aspects that makes us vulnerable and also compassionate. Thus the discussion of how to separate out the emotional responses we feel and that happens faster than thought is critical to the development of our intuitive and insightful skills. To be clear, emotional response is not intuitive insight. Intuitive insight might cause an emotional response but they are not the same. Significant emotional response clouds the information you will receive. Significant emotional response acts in a way that is similar to the static noise on a phone so that you do not get a clear sense of the information which is being shared.

A critical factor in the development of the intuitive skills is the ability to separate out emotion from information so that the information may be shared accurately and clearly and without judgment. Another issue in the development of the intuitive skills is that the unconscious part of the self which is part of the system which is receiving the intuitive information will try and please you. In the process the unconscious will often share images from earlier experiences where you were pleased with the information you received.

Thus you may see a series of images etc that you have seen before. The person acting to receive the intuitive information must be able to clear out these types of noise.

Definition of emotion

Emotion may be defined in medical terms, in humanistic terms and in structured logic. For our purposes we will consider emotion both a feeling state and a response which produces a feeling state which is often strong and which may arise faster than thought. It is often produced as a limbic system response and may include physiological and behavioral changes in the body.

How are your emotions experienced?

No one has a complete understanding of how emotions are processed or how the memories of situations to which you have an emotional response are stored. Neuroscience and research into the limbic and polyvagal system has given us a number of clues as mentioned above but the information is still incomplete. In addition to neurological, limbic and polyvagal processes, both regular memories and muscle memory clearly play a part in the process of experiencing, expressing and storing emotion. Likewise smell, taste, sound and physical setting can all impact our emotional experience.

In this process of exploring emotion and intuition we are particularly interested in how to experience emotion and separate those emotional moments from insight and intuition. It is important to clear emotion that is present, remembered or stored during the intuitive experience. Emotion can cloud the information which is received. Emotion can cause a person to suppress important information. Emotion can cause a person to justify to themselves the sharing of information in a way where the information is no longer in truth.

So how do you personally experience emotion? What are the predominant ways in which you have emotional experiences? Would you describe yourself as a calm person? An angry person? A rational person? A sad person? A depressed person? An optimistic person? Take a moment and pull out a small notebook that you can fit in your pocket. Carry it for the next 24 hours and note down each time you have a significant emotional response. See what kinds you actually have.

Then check in with a few friends. How would they describe you? Ask three or more people to describe what your most common emotional responses are to daily life. Then ask one or two family members or the equivalent the same question. Notice your emotional responses to what they say and note all the information which they share with you down in the notebook. You are building a snapshot of both internal and external emotional behavior which as we move through this process you will use to help you develop clarity and accuracy in your intuitive information.

DEFENSIVE PATTERNS

Emotional experiences can cause us to use defensive responses to life situations. These defensive responses can be verbal, physical or may extend into what some people see as the energetic/extended part of human consciousness. These responses may include things like yelling, making a snarky comment, stomping feet, throwing something, brooding, withdrawing, changing body position, shaking etc. When we engage in a defensive response, current physiological theory supports the idea that we are protecting the "self" or the "core part of the persona."

For our discussion, the recognition that we have engaged a defense response and recognition of the type of defensive response in which we are engaged is important. Once you recognize you have engaged a defensive response you can begin to learn the following" 1. What are your triggers? 2. Why did you feel the need to trigger? 3. Should you have triggered or is this an automatic or "left-over from another situation" response? 4. Is your emotional or physical response bigger than the situation really calls for? 5. How might you interrupt your defensive response in the future? What new choice of behavior are you going to make when you recognize that you have triggered and you are in defense? How will you implement that choice in daily life?

Once you recognize the defense is engaged you can also determine the types of defensive patterns you are using most often. This recognition allows you greater insight into when you might use a defensive pattern in the future. This is something important to recognize because when you are in defense you are not in the mode to receive intuitive information. Nor do flashes of insight happen as often as one would like when in defense. If one wishes to accurately access intuitive information being sure that one is not in defense is an important step in the process.

Finally, what are some of the interventions you can use to interrupt your personal defensive responses?

1. Ground, center and align. This interrupts the defensive response.
2. Breath and switch your focus to a different thought.
3. Breath in the word "grace" and breath out the word "compassion."
4. Do a remembering moment where you deliberately remember a joyous experience or an experience when you felt gratitude.
5. Send the energy of the defensive response into the ground. Let it drain out of the body.

Now see if you can create several other interventions which you might use to interrupt your patterned responses. Be sure to write them down. Let an act of creation begin the process of helping you to create a stronger and less swayed center of yourself.

Emotional response
is faster than thought

Science has found that hormonal responses and the overall responses of the limbic system are faster responses than that of thought. So for example, you may want to have a happy day and you wake up angry at the world. There is no logical reason why you feel angry. You just do. Well, during the night, food that you have eaten, dreams you may have had, memories of the experiences of the past few days, have all been shown to cause changes in the limbic system response. Because you feel angry, you may snap out your verbal responses to any questions that come your way. Or you might yell at a family member without a good reason. Or you might be unable to organize what you want to take to work or you may drive too fast in your car. In a calm and quiet moment you may feel surprised that you took these actions. They are not "who you are." They are not behaviors in which you generally engage. But you may be responding to the biochemical actions of the body.

Another example: if you are really angry but do not want to hit anyone, you might hit them anyway because the hitting response happens faster than the thought "I do not want to hit this person. I just want to walk away." Controlling the angry response can be very difficult. That does not mean you do not work at it until you do develop the skills so that you do not hit another person. No matter the justification, if you are doing the hitting the problem is with you and not with the person you are striking out toward. Having a fast response just means that it may take a great deal of dedicated practice to rewire the body's responses.

Yet another example: if you are really sad and do not want to cry in front of others, the tears may still start flowing down your cheeks because the body's response happens faster than the thought "I will not cry in front of anyone."

Healing through emotional expression

There appear to be a number of different ways in which emotions may be experienced and possibly be cleared. Dialogue, listening, an act of creation such as writing music or a book, participating in sports, climbing a mountain, setting a goal for the self and achieving it, and experiencing nature are all among the possibilities. Consider watching for a more significant/powerful emotional response during the next few days. Look for an emotional experience that is in excess of what would be considered an appropriate level of response for the situation. Then try one of the methods listed like writing a book or in a journal, going on a serious hike or watching a sunset and see what your response is to the action. write directly about your experience. Be as honest and complete as you are able to be. Keep in mind that the greater the emotional response the more electrical charge may be stored in the body. In general, you want an action that moves an equal amount of energy to the level of charge in the emotional experience. A creative act which takes a great deal of learning or focus usually expends the most amount of energy. If you have never painted a picture, you might try. If you have never run a marathon you might try training for one. If you have never learned to break-dance you might try learning some of the moves. If you have never learned to do yoga, qi gong or meditate you might give it a try.

Take a moment now and make a list of ways that you have cleared an emotional response in the past. That information is valuable as you develop your tool kit. Keep in mind that what works in one situation may not work in another so having multiple methods with which to appropriately express emotion and clear excess emotional response is valuable. As you review the ways in which you have cleared notice the physical situations in which the process worked and notice the emotions you were feeling leading up to the change so that you can use that method if and when you encounter a similar experience.

GROUNDING AS THE START

There are many different ways to engage in what is popularly and esoterically called "Grounding." In grounding through visualization, breath, directed thought, meditation, sports exercise, or dance (to name a few of the options) one engages to link the physical body to the 7 Hz current which is naturally produced by the Earth. The hope in "grounding" is to move the body into a receptive state where the current which flows freely over the surface of the Earth also flows freely into and over the body. Many people have a physical, sensate response to these visualization/meditation experiences. These physical experiences are reported to include: Feeling pulled down into the earth, feeling heavy - so heavy that one cannot pick up their legs, feeling connected to all the physical objects present, and feeling a surge of power throughout the body. While your experience of grounding will be unique to your body, do notice your physical sensate reactions as you go through one or more of these methods of grounding.

It should be noted that there are many methods of grounding and many methods of meditation that have been made present for thousands of years. If you know a method of grounding which is not listed here and with which you are comfortable you may certainly use it in this process. However, please distinguish between methods where you ground into the heart vs. where you ground into the Earth.

For the purposes of this process you must ground into the Earth. Also, there are a number of traditional and esoteric methods of grounding into the Earth through the tail bone. While this is a perfectly good method and a great deal of current can be received it should be noted that the tail bone is one inch in diameter at best where as the feet are much larger and the base of the corona which wraps the body is larger yet.

So for our purposes using something with more area in which to receive the available earth 7 Hz current is more viable. Below are several methods for accessing this "grounding" body feeling:

Method 1:

This is a basic method of grounding and may be used by anyone who wishes.

1. Breathe in for a count of 4 and out for a count of 4 three times.
2. Feel your feet on the floor. Are they warm or cold?
3. Allow your feet to feel heavy and solid against the floor.
4. Then using your breath to let go of your feet allow the image of your feet falling through the ground all the way on to the surface of the iron core at the center of the Earth.
5. Allow the warmth of that connection to slide over the surface of the skin and sink into all the cells of the body as that warmth moves up the body.

Method 2:

This is a second basic method of grounding where you align yourself to the perceived consciousness of the Earth.

1. Allow yourself to recognize how you are breathing.
2. Let the breath become gentle and relaxed.
3. Using visualization as a tool to guide body response, see the legs becoming heavy and falling into the Earth.
4. See them slide into the center of the core of the Earth.
5. Breathe and reach out your consciousness much as if you were reaching out your hand to touch the shoulder of a friend and touch the consciousness of the Earth.

6. Allow yourself to receive the current which is gifted to you from this contact with the earth into your physical feet.
7. Let this earth current sink into the tissues of the body.

Method 3:

This is a heart-centered method which still grounds through the base of the field.

1. Breathe and become aware of your heart beating in your chest.
2. Take a second gentle breath and see if you can feel your heart actually beat.
3. Then with the next breath follow the breath into the lungs.
4. Then with the next breath follow the breath all the way into the heart.
5. Then feel a current from the heart traveling down the body and into the legs and from there into the feet.
6. Now follow that current down into the Earth, all the way to the core of the earth, breathing into your heart and into the heart of the earth.
7. Become aware of the consciousness of the Earth, and give a gift of gratitude of your heart light to the Earth as a thank you for the cherishing of your body and your life.
8. Then receive the corresponding gift back along the heart current and into your physical feet and upwards throughout the body tissue.
9. Allow any excess charge to spill out of the head and back down into the core of the earth, once again honoring the earth.

METHOD 4:

This is an esoteric method of grounding where you anchor the physical form in time and space to 4 directions. This is reported to allow individuals to move forward and backward in time with greater reliability and security.

1. Using imagination as a tool to guide the process, see your feet falling into the core of the earth, then sink the base of your body corona (the charged field which wraps around your body) into the Earth.
2. Reach up from the core into the center point in the center of the belly/tien tien and move a current of the Earth current up through the heart and then up through the top of the head to the point of individuation and into a connection with the Divine.
3. Then sink a tendril of light from the sun to the front of the heart.
4. Then sink a tendril of light from the moon to the back of the heart.
5. Allow the currents of light to move in each direction so that you have twisted all of the strands together and they move up and down the mid-line power current of the body.
6. Allow any excess current to fountain out of the top of the head and flow over the surface of the body back into the earth, so that you are standing as a virtual link between heaven and Earth.

DRAINING EXCESS EMOTION

Excess emotion, an emotional response which is bigger than the situation warrants, is rarely useful. Taking and having control of that excess emotion is an important step in the process of developing body awareness and body management. It is important to distinguish the fact that excess emotional current is different than grounded current. The spectrographic map of various hormones ranges upwards from 20 Hz. Again, grounded current is 6.8 to 7 Hz. You are literally responding to a different range of frequencies. Because current moves faster at higher frequencies it can cancel out or overwhelm your perception of waves that are running at lower rates. So in addition to grounding, learning how to drain off emotional over charge may be a valuable process to learn.

Method 1:
This is a basic method of reducing overcharge in an emotional response by using breath.
1. If you begin to feel fear, rage sorrow or any excess emotion, shift your focus to your breath.
2. Feel the breath entering the body.
3. Feel the air flow down your nose, your throat and into the lungs.
4. Feel the lungs fill.
5. Allow the body to relax as your exhale.
6. Bring your mind back to feeling the breath each time it drifts in its focus.
7. Repeat.

Method 2:
Excess emotion often happens faster than thought. This is a method of training your body to have an automatic response to excess emotion and draining it off so the physical and verbal actions that follow the experience can be more

controlled. This method is particularly useful for people who have raised teenagers!

1. Begin with the breath. Now exhale and try to clear out the breath fully. This will require a little extra push from your belly. Kind of like a grunt.
2. Then just as you would when a teenager comes home at midnight instead of the agreed upon 10pm, let your body move into the form where you "put your foot down."
3. Then release and let the excess emotion drain right out of the body into the ground.

METHOD 3:

In an emergency, excess emotion can often be converted into charge which can be used to help and not harm. If the body perceives something as an emergency when it is not, then that charge needs to be converted another way. This method uses the gathering action of getting ready to make a response as a mechanism toward giving the self a moment of time to think and then make a choice for what you wish to do with the charged you have created. This method is important to drill in non-essential situations so that a body habit pattern becomes engaged and can be used.

1. Perceive when the body is gathering charge.
2. Locate where the charge is occurring in the body.
3. Make a conscious choice where you want to send the energy so that you do not harm anyone including yourself.
4. Take a belly breath and with the exhale send the energy in the direction you have chosen.
5. Repeat until the full charge is released.

6. Consciously relax the muscles/body in the area that charged originally.
7. Breathe into the belly and exhale slowly three times to fully clear.

CENTERING AND ALIGNING

Centering and aligning are the next steps in a complete grounding process. They allow you to move back into truth using visualization and body sensing. Doing both of the exercises below, at least once a day, allows the body to maintain a level of connectedness and allows the self to be more connected to the truth of who you are as an individual. It can also be used anytime one is being swayed by both positive or negative experiences. Remember that all these exercises are focused on helping you to access truth throughout your day no matter that current "life moment" circumstance.

CENTER:

Bring Earth energy through feet, legs, pelvis, torso, heart, up to shoulders, then let it flow down arms and hands and at the same time up through neck and head. Then let it flow out through top of head and fountain/cascade down over body to Mother Earth. This creates a rinsing away process to clear the body. Let the excess charge, flow down to Mother Earth and give the noise that has rinsed out of the body as a gift to her so that she can experience what you have experienced.
Connect to your heart.
Feel the energy moving up and down the midline power current.

ALIGN:
Connect to the center of the self and the truth of your existence. Use statements that are truthful like "my address is ...", "my given name is...", or other factual statements.
Align your body with that truth.

LET THE HEART OPEN
My grandmother used to say "it is wise never to throw out the baby with the bath water", so when we wish to receive information from the intuitive process, a piece of the emotional response which can and should be used on a regular basis, is letting the heart open in appreciation and gratitude for the information. In addition, any information received must always be shared with the heart engaged but in a neutral place.

Deliberately opening the heart when you receive information is just good manners. It is a way to say "thank you." Always remember that when individuals come to you for insight, the information which you share with them has weight and potentially power. It must be shared accurately, with wisdom and with discernment. Having the heart open as you share allows you to better discern how the information is being received so that you may impart information with great appreciation and consideration of the individual in front of you.

CHAPTER TWO

WHAT IS INTUITION?

The next step in this journey is to discover our personal capacity for intuition, tune that capacity, separate out our emotional response and be able to share information from a place of truth and compassion.

DEFINITION OF INTUITION
Intuition can be defined as an instinctive response rather than more conscious and direct forms of thinking or reasoning. It often appears to be an immediate response and can include a sort of all encompassing or total knowing type experience.

WHERE DOES INTUITIVE INFORMATION COME FROM
No one knows where intuitive information comes from. In the laboratory we have been able to see that there are specific, identifiable and consistent brain responses which correspond to receipt of intuitive information. But the origin of that information is still an unknown. It may be that the body and the memory system are incorporating information at an unconscious level. It may be that we are being gifted information from the larger cosmos. There may be a form of universal unconscious which humans can access. While the origins of intuitive information remain unknown, most skilled intuitives will tell you one of two things about where

there information comes from: that they can feel the information coming into a specific point in their head or that they think up, toward their perception of the Divine and the information flows back down.

HOW DOES INTUITION PRESENT ITSELF

Many people who wish to develop their intuitive skills have read books on the subject, watched others use their skills or had experiences of intuitive response. As a result they will often have very definite ideas about how the information will appear and exactly what form it will take. As such, these ideas may be limited to what they have read or seen. Intuitive information comes in many different ways. It can appear using senses or information pathways which one does not expect. Some of the varied pathways are listed below. How many different ways have you personally experienced an intuitive insight? See if you can add to the list below of possible pathways.

The unconscious tries to communicate with each of us. It appears that a part of the job of the unconscious. It is as a part of your emergency response system. It is an early warning system for all kinds of danger. And since we each have individual experiences, the vocabulary which your personal unconscious uses will be unique to you. The images which it sends you, the sounds that you hear, the smells which you smell when receiving information will be specific to your personal intuitive vocabulary. So you will want to write down in your notebook your list of personal vocabulary equivalents. For example: if you get an intuitive flash with an image of your father in your personal vocabulary it may mean that the person is dealing with "daddy" stuff. Another example: might be hearing a jingle from a commercial. A specific phrase from that jingle might have meaning in the situation. Yet another example: smelling sugar cookies baking - if that is a good memory for you - it might be that the situation you will be addressing is linked to a good memory. If it is a bad memory for you because you burnt the cookies - it might mean that something is literally going to burn.

Learn to identify the vocabulary and metaphors with which the unconscious communicates. You will find it will improve the accuracy of the information you receive and it will speed the development of your skills.

Memory

The intuitive and the unconscious use memories to share a variety of types of information with the more conscious mind as the linkage to the conscious mind is already physically in place.

The types of information generally include the following:

1. Situations of learning which need to be resolved.
2. Information which matches experiences that one has had in the past and that has a key nugget that is relevant to the information which the unconscious is trying to share with the conscious mind.
3. Specific parts of images like color, physical setting or people who are once again involved.
4. A situation which will take place at the same time of year.

What intuitive information your unconscious is trying to communicate takes practice to recognize.

For example: when you see images of children playing baseball it could be that the unconscious it trying to communicate "summer play", "a specific baseball game and an experience related to that game", "an experience that happened while watching baseball", or "an interpersonal interaction having to do with sports." Making a list of possible information with a short description of how you felt physically and emotionally will aid you in more rapid recognition of the actual meaning and will also assist in developing your personal vocabulary with your unconscious. There will always be some direct relationship to the informational response you are trying to access.

SOUND BYTES

Sound, in particular alert/emergency sounds and pieces of songs are common methods with which intuitive information is communicated. For example: my bank recently closed it's local branch. I needed a new bank that met my specific requirements. I looked at a number of banks in the local area but was not finding what I wanted. Then as I was driving past a shopping center in the local area I heard a jingle I had sung for a commercial. "... that's my bank" was the lyric which played in my head. I did not know there was a bank in that shopping center. I drove in, found the bank, got information on the bank and it was indeed what I was looking for.

Another example: Every time I would walk past an electrical switch in my kitchen I would hear a snapping sound. It made no sense. The lights worked fine. Then one day we had a short because I was running too many things in the kitchen at once. I got an electrician out to upgrade and correct things and as an after thought I asked him to look at the light switch. It turned out that it was an electrical short that was triggering my intuition into making that snapping sound in my head. It was a fire waiting to happen.

Make a list over the course of a week of each of the pieces of songs, commercial jingles, whistles, snaps etc which you hear in your head as part of your daily life and see if they relate in any way to what was happening in your life at the time. Again, you may want to add this information to the list of vocabulary you are identifying as ways that your intuitive response and unconscious are trying to communicate with you.

SMELLS

Smells are one of the oldest and strongest senses that we have as humans. When you receive a specific smell in the process of seeking intuitive information pay close attention to it. Again, pay attention to the context. Has the smell come as part of an image? Has the smell occurred spontaneously as you are doing a daily task? Has the smell happened when you are around a specific place which does not fit the environment?

An example of an intuitive episode that includes smell might be: I was driving past a building that had been shuttered for some period of time. But for the last three days I got images of my dogs at dinner time and I kept smelling blood. I finally decided to pay attention and stopped at that house. I called out to see if anyone was there and was rewarded by a bark. I walked around the side of the house into the alley and there was a dog who was hooked by his collar on the chain link fence. He was clearly in distress. I loaded him up in the car, took him home, fed and watered him and checked our local posting of missing animals that are put on our rural mailboxes. He went home that evening.

Another example that appears to be more common across individuals is that intuitive images will come with the smell of dust or mud and blood. In both cases it often is the case that the images received are related to very old episodes.

Consider listing smells that have no reason to be in a particular place or associated with a particular situation which you perceive over the course of a week. List the environment and what you were thinking about at the time. How does this information enrich the vocabulary list you are creating? What kind of additional information does it give you? Do some careful thinking about the specific situations in which the information came to you. See if you can notice similar situations over the next month. Are you getting information in those similar situations? If so, be sure to develop a habit of checking in with your sense of smell to see what information it may give you.

TASTES

Like smell, taste is one of our oldest senses. Despite the standard limits of sweet, sour, bitter and salty of our taste buds, extended sensing can give you many more specifics within the context of taste. When having intuitive experiences there are common reports of things like "the taste of dust" linked to historic imagery. Tastes of gun powder, metal and mud have been linked to battles. Tastes of sugar or sweet tastes are often linked to celebrations. The taste of particular foods are often linked to memories which will have elements of significance and relevance to the individual requesting knowledge.

Again the development of a personal vocabulary of tastes can provide information which is valuable. One does need to be cautious in the interpretation of the information. Provide the specifics of the tastes to the person with whom you are sharing. Do not interpret the information. You will also want to always check the taste of any information which becomes clear in your awareness as taste may provide time frame, emotional context and other information of value.

Floating Images

Not all imagery will be clearly defined. It is not unusual just prior to more complete information coming into ones awareness that random images will appear. These images are often warning or warm up signals. They tend to give very specific information when linked to the more complete intuitive sensing but when taken out of context have little meaning and appear truly random.

Not all humans appear to have this type of intuitive sensing response. It is more common in individuals who have long suppressed their skills as they become more aware. It is also a common form of sensing which hunters seem to develop over time. For example a hunter might sense in the following way: just prior to finding a group of deer in the forest, the hunter will know which direction to look as the floating image will appear and cause them to look in that direction.

Another form of the floating image is a form of noise. Instead of happening as a lead up to a more complete flow of information, these images appear when information transfer stalls. The stalling occurs when the information which is being shared is deemed by the conscious mind as wrong and the information is denied. Then the unconscious gives a series of floating images as a way to please the conscious. It often involves messages that were correct and successfully imparted real information in the past.

Become aware of the timing of floating images. When they happen at the beginning of a more complete information sharing they carry specific relevance. When they happen after a stalling of information go back to the information which you denied as it will generally be found to be correct.

The Flash

An intuitive "flash" or "hit" is among the most common ways in which people sense information. This form of information sharing through the unconscious is usually both specific in one or more details/elements presented and is complete in the information which it is trying to impart. This type of information sharing comes in a fraction of a second. The challenge of this type of information is that in our busy and complex lives we see the information, recognize it for a moment as significant and then drop the ball. Most of us do not take the time to write the information down and in the midst of daily life simple forget that the information has been made available.

It is important to carry a small notebook with which to make notes on experiences such as this type in the beginning of intuitive development and practice, as it will help the intuitive to strengthen the pathways through which accurate and complete information is distributed. Simply writing down time and topic can be enough to help you further develop this type of connection. And if one is in a difficult or complex profession, where lives are dependent on accurate information, having a clear accurate channel to this information can save lives. Knowing when to duck and when to move can be critical in an emergency.

THE AHA MOMENT

Intuitive information which comes as insight into how our life experience unfolds and the meaning which our life holds, provides us a way to move forward with our life from a place of greater enrichment and compassion. The AhHa moment in which we receive this type of information supports our development as a person. It is information which is valuable to us personally and in general is not as relevant to our parishioners/clients. It is a complete information insight which we are meant to put into practice in our daily lives.

Take some time over a period of a week and see if you have any moments that provide you insight into how to better live your life. Note each of these down in your notebook. Spend ten minutes thinking about each episode and determine if there are actions you can take to make your life work better as a result of these AhHa moments. Do all of these moments follow a particular theme? Do all of these moments come with information which will help you to change ingrained behaviors? Do any or all of these moments show you methods of organizing your life to greater effect?

Pay attention to the topic, the type of insight, the physical place you receive the information and how you were feeling just prior to receiving the information. Make notes on all of the above since again, you can develop a pathway to access information in the future which provides personally relevant and supportive insights. Since we all experience periods of change in our lives, being able to access supportive information with which to move through periods of great change and stress with greater grace and serenity is important. Begin to develop these connections now and you will have access the rest of your life.

River of information

We live in a sea of energy. This sea of energy has currents that provide us information at varying frequency rates. One of the ways in which information can come to us is in a "river" or "continuous flow." This river of information is not a single image repeating nor does it come in a flash of a second. This is a more sustained insight. The information comes as if we are observing a panorama or landscape of the parishioners/client's experience. It will contain a broad range of information which will be relevant to the person and will include things like relationships, things the person is to learn, areas of discomfort in their life and areas of extreme distortion in belief patterns.

Most of the information which a practitioner receives in this way will never be shared with the parishioner/client. The challenge for the practitioner is to select the information which will provide the most benefit to the person. Remember the rules of sharing confidential information as you select what you will share. (See Appendix A) In general it is wise to select what is most relevant to the immediate needs of the person. If you have been working with a parishioner/client long term, then sharing small specific single pieces of wisdom discerned from the river of information may be appropriate but be conservative. Often the river of information insights you will receive will be powerful pieces of information that can hurt or help depending on how the information is being shared with the person. Be gentle and kind!

A COMPLETE FORM OR DIRECT KNOWING

Similar to the flash experience, an experience of direct knowing comes as a single unit of experience and contains all of the necessary information at one time. The difference is in the way the information comes. Rather than a flash of intuition and perception which is "seen" by the individual, it is information which comes in a direct channel from the Divine. It enters this dimension and frequency range through a connection point between individuated incarnation and the larger all at the edge of the tenth layer of the biofield. The information flows down the midline power current of the body and seats in the brain area first and over a period of a few seconds expands to take in the whole of the body. Where the "flash" experience is the unconscious putting together relevant information combined with unconscious information and perception the "direct knowing" experience comes from outside the individuated incarnation.

When one is seeking a direct knowing experience in order to address complex situations with comprehensive solutions, one must reach up and establish the connection to the Divine first, in whatever form is appropriate to the individual incarnation and then pose the fullest and most complete question including all known aspects of information. Then one waits and breathes. Within a short period of time, after stillness of the mind has been established, the information will come.

It is wise to look at all of the information received in this fashion as it is usually complex and nuances within the information can be lost when not explored fully. Often a minimum period of at least several hours and preferably several days, should pass prior to taking action on information received through direct knowing.

Moments of disorientation or disconnection

When you are seeking intuitive information and you have moments of disorientation or disconnection which either interrupts or happens slightly before the information arrives, ground, ground and reground. This reaction is usually as a result of something in the images being acutely stressful to see. It may be a disconnection in the belief system of the practitioner who is receiving the information or it may simply be images too painful or horrific to want to see. It can be difficult to see one starvation after the next war after the next murder after the next agony. Remember to be patient with yourself. Ground, center, align and hold compassion for yourself and if you were seeking information for another, hold grace and compassion for them as well.

If the experience of disorientation happens on a regular basis, this is not imagery causing an issue but instead something physiological which needs to be properly explored and addressed. Keep in mind that while this work is both controversial and complex, it needs to be grounded in daily activities that are solidly realistic. A continuous process of testing the truth of your experiences and the accuracy of your experiences is necessary. Without a commitment to the groundedness of daily life, the demand for internal truth and the continuous development of the skills, it is unwise to follow this path, as more negatives could be created in one's life than value created from it. There is spiritual value in doing laundry, feeding the dog, scrubbing the floor, and making a good meal when consciousness is brought to the process and love is shared in every interaction. These things keep the balance of one's life when one is seeking the larger and more complex skills of intuition and knowing.

LISTENING TO THE QUIET INNER VOICE

This can be called the "oou" factor. "OOU" you might see something you do not like. "OOU" you might see something you do like! Astounding as it seems many people ignore or actively dismiss as wrong the promptings of their inner voice on matters of importance. Often the inner voice provides a warning or information which is not welcome. Make a choice to actively listen to the inner voice for a week. Write down each time the information comes through. The action is low level awareness, higher level awareness, recognition, stopping the dismissal, recognition of the information, allowing the uncomfortable feelings to happen alongside the recognition of the information, then instituting a change of behavior. Recognize, hear and listen, then make a choice to change or not change the situation.

Allowing yourself to act on what you hear when the internal voice is quiet

You have noticed information coming through. Now what? In many individuals just recognizing that information is available is the most difficult part. Many of us have dismissed the information we are receiving as fast as it is comes to us. So allowing the information to come to consciousness, even when it is uncomfortable is an important first step. Remember, if the information is contrary to what you want to take place, denial of the information is a sure way to make it happen. Instead, recognize that the information you have just received is situational. It is the best information you have at that moment. BUT the causes are not all made! Since the information has come in advance of the situation, the situation can be changed! So instead of following the pattern in our society of denial of truth, look at what is the truth at that moment, decide if that is what you want to make manifest or if you want to make a change. Then let the situation unfold or make changes as necessary.

Noticing your disregard

One of the most difficult aspects of learning to pay attention to your intuition and flashes of insight is to learn to pay attention on the occasions when you would automatically dismiss the information without any exploration or focus. It is hard to interrupt that habit pattern. And in most people it is a habit pattern. And if you wish to follow this path this habit pattern needs to be interrupted so that you at least stop for a moment and recognize that some information has been made present.

Consider spending several days focusing on when information comes through as the natural process of a day. Write that information down. Then pick one of the times that information generally comes through and pay direct attention to when and under what circumstances, you simply ignore the information. Write down on the same page under that time period, the type of information which came through. Write down if that information was useful. Make note of how many times in that period information is made available to you. List the type of information and the frequency of that type of information in that time period. Then select another time period and repeat this process.

Many people find that certain types of information come in at certain times of day or during certain types of activities. If you pay direct attention, you can see if you get repeat information. Then you can map the type of information that you most often ignore.

NOTICING NOT WANTING TO HEAR

Once you notice the type of information you most often ignore, do some thinking about situations in the past that might have caused you to make that choice. Ask yourself, "is it still the right choice for me to ignore this type of information?" If it is then continue to ignore the information. If it has a use in your life consider spending one day a week in that time period or activity paying specific attention to the information which comes through. Write the information down. Intuitive information can be easy to forget in a life that is busy.

Try to follow through the change in focus for at least three months. It often can take that long a period of time to make a behavioral change and make it successfully.

A number of individuals who have tried this process have found that they were ignoring information which was related to a painful life episode or to situations which they felt they could not change.

With a painful life episode you might consider following this process:

STEP 1:
How would you have handled the situation differently given the information which you have today?

STEP 2:
Determine how you might forgive yourself for making the choice you made.

STEP 3:
Determine if there are any resources you need to establish so that if the situation happens again you can make a different and possibly more successful choice.

STEP 4:
Put those resources in place.

STEP 5:
Commit an act of forgiveness toward self. For example: buy flowers for your self. Go on a enjoyable hike. Meditate on a sunrise.

STEP 6: Appreciate that you are able to make a new choice.

HEALING THROUGH INTUITION WITH WISDOM

Another option is to use your developing intuitive skills to create healing for yourself. You might want to create a ceremony to celebrate a change in your focus and use some of your intuitive information to guide you while you develop the ceremony. You might want to write in a journal the experience you have had in the recognition process and allow yourself to sit with a blank page and see if any related intuitive information becomes available. Write it down and see how it relates to the issue you are addressing. Or you might want to commit an act of creation. Paint a painting, write a book, write a play, choreograph a dance, and in whatever medium you choose allow your developing intuitive skills to come out and play!

In whatever option you choose make a distinct behavioral change. And give yourself both the gift of sufficient time and plan the process of noticing so that you will be successful. For many people changing habit patterns is challenging. Remember to be as compassionate with yourself as you would be with others you might be helping.

CHAPTER THREE

WHAT IS COMPASSION?

When addressing emotion and intuition and the development of intuitive skills, compassion in three primary areas is an integral part of the process. First, compassion is necessary as a part of empathy in how you share the information which you receive through the intuitive process. Second, compassion with appropriate boundaries is critical in how you make judgments on what are reasonable actions to take in support of your parishioners/clients. Third, compassion is necessary when sharing information to which you parishioner/client may have a significant negative response.

Compassion in spiritual terms is often seen as an act that is a recognition of the needs of another. Further, it is often combined with the recognition that if the situation were slightly changed the person with the ability to support the person challenged, could instead be the person challenged. "There but for the grace of the Divine go I" is real. The act of recognition of need which then results in taking an action and giving a person what they want or need or finding a solution when they are in difficulty is the compassionate action. It is linked to recognition of need, and that action of providing support and doing so from a place of generosity. Compassion is often confused with generosity in the action of giving an individual what they want. The action of just giving a person what they want is not compassion and does not support an individual long term. Often people forget that teaching a person to fish is far more valuable to the person long term than just giving them a fish for that night's dinner.

At the same time compassion is an important piece of the glue which helps us to repair wrongs which have been done by circumstance and accident. The drive to make right what has been wrong is an important action to take from a spiritual perspective.

Definition of compassion

Compassion is a form of sympathy. We will define compassion as being aware of, recognizing and wanting to help remedy the misfortunes of others through having deep sympathy, empathy, appropriate boundaries and the urge to take action.

How does one create calm-passion

Acts of compassion and the recognition of a need for compassion begin with a personal spiritual connection. Compassion is an act of empathy where we see the pain and difficulty experienced by another and without having to experience it directly as a personal learning, we seek to correct a perceived wrong. Compassion is first established through the experience of right and wrong. The wave in truth or the wave in distortion. From a place of calm and spiritual connection, perceiving the correctness of a situation is possible. Much like being able to hear the static noise on a cell phone, when one is calm and connected, the static noise of an incorrect situation becomes clear as an emotional response in the urge to take action on other's behalf.

Once the connection is made to the issue, situation or objective then a recognition of the personal level of passion to aid in the resolution of the wrongness and bring it back into alignment with truth is assessed. That level of passion is what carries us forward in the long term and allows us to address a need within the level of scope created by our passion.

WHERE DOES A SPIRITUAL CONNECTION FIT?

True compassion comes from a combination of the recognition of something that needs repair, a spiritual connection, gratitude, and wisdom. Spiritual connection allows us to see the value which is woven into each and every beautiful work of art which is a person.

The calm spiritual connection can be created in a number of different ways. The first is the most mechanical. Brain research has found a still point of thought that can be created through the process of doing neurofeedback. When this still point is achieved, in that moment an act of creation can be brought forth that allows for rightness to be re-established.

Another way is to pray or meditate until a deep connection to the issue is established and path forward is seen. Yet another is to simply see a need and a solution through a flash of insight. And another is to recognize a need in the self to take action to create value in the world and seek an opportunity to take that action.

It is not sufficient to right a wrong. One must think of the long term consequences of ones actions. For to simply right a wrong in the moment, without creating a path to wholeness, is a bit like giving an addict money and not caring if they spend it on drugs instead of the food their body so desperately needs.

THE QUESTION OF KARMA AND REDEMPTION

Compassion is an integral part of the process of separation of emotion and intuition since compassion, when it is not understood correctly, causes us to use emotions to override the information coming from our intuitive recognition. The need to care and cherish can be so strong that wisdom is not properly applied in the moment. Wisdom must be applied to balance compassion. One of the forms which wisdom may take is the recognition of the karma or life experience of the individuals involved and the paths to redemption or resolution which are possible.

This brings us to karma and life experience. Karma, as a word in popular speech, is often misused and misunderstood. In the simplest form karma, is the sum total of the causes/actions (thought, word and deed) that one has made in their life time. Their total life experience. This includes both positive and negative actions.

Karma can also be broken into more complex parts:
1. Personal Karma: Individuals total life experience.
2. Family-line Karma: The combined experiences of all the members of one family.
3. Group Karma: The combined experiences of a group of individuals.

4. Poly-Karma: The actions and non-actions which are arising from the combined actions/non-actions of all.

Karma is relevant to the discussion of compassion because our ability to distinguish a good choice from a negative choice is related to how much wisdom we use in that moment. The amount of wisdom available to us is infinite. How much we choose to access is often related to the positive and negative value we have created in our life. In other words our karma. When we have an understanding that before we commit an act of compassion based on either an emotional or intuitive response, we need to use the maximum wisdom available to us to discern the correct action to take for our lives and the lives of our parishioners/clients, we then move from a place where maximum value may be created for all involved.

In the creation of situations which result in value for all those involved through the use of intuitive information there is often an aspect of correction or redemption in the actions being taken. Wisdom which aids us in choosing the correct words, the correct weight of the words we use to share information and the amount of information which we share, allow for situations which have been out of balance to be brought back into balance.

The creation of balance can be interpreted as a form of redemption. By taking this action of sharing intuitive information you are also providing a new definition of the situation. You are bringing the situation you are addressing back in to balance "redeeming" the situation. Thus the act of compassion, which is integral to the act of the sharing of intuitive information, becomes an act of redemption when the intuitive information is applied with wisdom.

How to do forgiveness of self

Often within the act of redemption is the act of forgiveness. Allowing yourself to see the information which you have denied even to yourself in the past, and being willing to share this information as accurately as possible in an effort to aid another is a powerful and positive action. Guilt over the times you have not listened to the self, denied information, or have worked against the self is not unusual. However, guilt is a useless emotion unless we use it to move ourselves forward into a better perception of ourselves and others by taking actions to resolve the guilt.

To resolve the guilt one must forgive oneself. The following steps are one way to take that action:

1. Look at the situations in which mistakes or poor choices were made.
2. Notice the choice points and the situation from which the issue arose.
3. Now look carefully at the choices and decide what you might do differently when faced with a similar situation.
4. How might that choice have effected the original situations outcome?
5. Spend a few minutes giving yourself permission to act in this new way if a similar situation ever shows up again.
6. Now judge the forgive-ability given that you have created new options for behavior, you have recognized the error(s) made, and you have given yourself the option to do something new.

7. Then allow yourself to stand in the connection you have established to the Divine and let the forgiveness from that source flow through you.
8. Offer appreciation to yourself and appreciation to all that is for the change you have just made.

How to forgive the other

Since life experience rarely happens in a void, it is not unusual to have to forgive others as well as ourselves. When you are sharing intuitive information, it may be resisted or denied. You may be criticized for the information which you have shared. You may be criticized for the form in which you shared the information, not immediately giving the person who is receiving the information exactly what they want. Strive to come to the process of the persons challenging response from the place of calm-passion. If you have shared the intuitive information from a place of truth and wisdom, then begin with a recognition that humans have a great deal of resistance to change.

This resistance to change can take many forms:
1. It can arise from the level of electrical resistance produced across physical tissue related to nervous system response.
2. The emotional, mental, and/or spiritual responses to the change when a highly charged issue arises.
3. Memories of similar life situations.
4. Or the naming of a truth which can be a relief and/or an immediate burden.
5. To that end, the ability to forgive the person receiving the information when they respond aggressively to intuitive

information which we have shared from a place of truth is important.

A similar process to the forgiveness of self can be used to forgive another with the key difference that first you must recognize that you are not responsible for another persons reactions. This is especially true when you have shared information from a place of truth, with the best wisdom on what to share, and ethics on how much to share, and consideration for the persons life situation. Recognition that change is hard for many people and that it is often easier to make others wrong than to pursue change in our own lives can also make the process of forgiveness easier.

Grant your parishioner/client a place of grace and forgiveness and release their response to your information into that grace. Remember to use appropriate boundaries, no blame, compassion in your dialogue and be sure your information is accurate prior to sharing the information.

CHAPTER FOUR

BASIC METHODS OF ACCESSING INTUITIVE INFORMATION

Intuitive information is only as good as the ability to access it. If you cannot access information when you need it, the information does not serve a useful purpose. Thus developing skills which produce reliable access to information as a first step and skills where the information itself is reliable is a solid second step. While there are as many ways to access the information as their are practitioners, having developed a specific and reliable pathway is valuable. Life is stressful and it is surprising the number of times that support can be requested of you under the most unusual circumstances. It is important to have a reliable method which provides information which is accurate. That takes practice.

While this book describes a set of steps which can be used to develop your intuitive skills there is no substitution for practice. These are skills, similar to learning to type or drive a car or parachuting. You must put in just as much time to learn these skills as you did learning to type or drive a car or jump out of a perfectly good airplane. There is no substitution for skills drill. There is no substitution for practicing methods to speak with people. There is no substitution for drilling until you have reliable accuracy in the information you receive and share.

Reaching up

Grounding, centering and aligning your heart to the Divine is the first process which should be used no matter what subsequent steps are used in reaching up to establish your intuitive connection. From there a logical next step is to deliberately reach up and connect into the Divine through the access point that is 3-22 feet above your head depending on the size of the biofield or corona which surrounds your body. In most people the access point is about 3-5 feet directly above the center point of the top of your head. To begin this process take a series of three deep breaths. One to relax, one to experience and one to focus. Then feel for the center point at the top of your head from inside your head. Once you establish the connection to the center point at the top of your head, then, using your creative mental aspect, see a line 90 degrees to the top of your head. Slide your consciousness up that line until you feel a small amount of pressure and perhaps hear a quiet pop sound. Then sink into contact with that point and reach for your connection to the Divine. Sink into contact with the Divine in whatever form is correct for your beingness and allow yourself joy and gratitude in the contact. Remember you can also reach from one point of space to any other point of space.

Allowing return flow of information

Once the connection is established it is important to actually allow the flow of information to come back into your consciousness. This is a surrender/allowing space. One surrenders to the will of the Divine and allows the information to slide back along the pathway you personally have established (so that you know the information is clean and safe to receive). Then you breathe and sit in allowing. See what information comes to consciousness.

At first, you may want to practice asking for information on an issue for yourself and for which you largely know the answers. In that way you can begin to test for accuracy, do not be nervous about the images and information which you will be getting back and get the connection established. Most people have to practice this several times prior to being able to get images immediately after they have received information. Lots of people take 24 to 48 hours to have the information come to consciousness when they start this practice. This is a skill. Skills must be drilled. This is just like learning to do scales at the piano. It does not come magically. It must be drilled.

With practice once a day each day for about 6 weeks most individuals can establish a connection which allows them to get and share information in a real time session with a client or parishioner. Remember the imagery will come in your personal unconscious/body vocabulary. Be careful not to interpret. State the images clearly and with precision.

REACHING INTO THE HEART

The method of "reaching into the heart" is a way that a kinesthetic may improve their accuracy and share what is truthful keeping to the actual limits of the information which they receive. It is a three step method. Again, one begins by grounding, centering and aligning. Next, one specifically aligns with the light of truth. Finally, one sinks into the center of the tips of the heart chakra. Wait in that connection until the images and colors which are being perceived become still.

Then you ask the question the person is seeking information about as precisely as possible of your own heart. See what kind of information you receive as a result. Only share the actual information which you perceive. Share no interpretations. Share no extra information and be sure that you are sitting in the light of truth in all of your sharing.

Aligning with the light of truth should be practiced for several weeks as a separate process before being used for an intuitive read. To align with the light of truth one begins with the breath. Take at least three breaths to clear your mind and begin to focus. Then using thought as a tool to direct the energy and focus make the connection to the Divine in whatever form is correct for you. Deepen your ground once the connection to the Divine is established. Then think about facts which are true about you. Things that are simple.

For example: your street address, your mothers name, your name, how old you are… Think about 20 facts and with each one send a pulse of energy using the breath and focus up to the Divine. Then feel and watch the flow of energy that comes back down to you along the same pathway. In a short period of time the flow of energy which comes back down will glow with the light of truth of the information which you have been sending up. Then sit in that flow of light and simply breathe and feel. How does that light feel on your skin? How does that light feel as it washes through your body and into the ground? In this process you are literally a link between the Divine and earth and aligning/sitting in truth as a practice place is very important for your ability to recognize the sensate experience of truth verses any other type of current flow.

Practice moving in and out of truth so that you can clearly feel when you are correctly aligned. This is a skill. You must drill this skill until you can link to the light of truth easily and comfortably. It generally takes several weeks of 10 min a day practice to establish a firm link. Give yourself the grace of time and do the skills drill. You will work better without feeling guilty because you cannot establish a connection. Instead move from a place of compassion and accuracy.

It is important that you be able to sit in the light of truth as you share information with your parishioners/clients. This will improve your accuracy, remove noise associated with images that are stored in your own field and strengthen your ability to support your parishioner/client. Remember all information needs to be shared with your parishioner/client according to ethical guidelines.

A caution, many kinesthetics do intuitive readings by feel. This is both positive and negative. To the positive the practitioner is sharing what they feel. To the negative most information when tested turns out to be unreliable, incomplete and inaccurate because it is being viewed through the filter of the practitioner's field. Often with the added limitation of sharing dogma instead of truth if they give old images or have difficulty accessing real information. If this is the preferred method of the practitioner, extra effort must be made to develop accuracy and reduce blind spots. Never share dogma. Only share what you actually perceived. In addition, those who believe they have an already established intuitive connection often do not discipline themselves to do the necessary skills drill. Do not fail those you are there to support at the very beginning. Learn your craft and do the skills drill.

Without adequate training in accuracy, the results of reading which is not based in truth, can be destructive. For example: a young practitioner was doing a reading in this way and they explained to the client, about whom they had no real knowledge, that "their father loved them and they were just like their father." This was both incorrect, as they did not have the serious mental health issues of their parent and devastating as that parent had been deeply abusive to them as a child. When the practitioner was questioned after the reading, they admitted that they felt the person needed reassurance about their parent and they had read that it was good to share that parents always love their children. While the intent of the practitioner was positive on the surface, when their behavior was explored more fully, it became evident that the practitioner had not disciplined themselves and done the necessary drill to become competent.

A practitioner must always be aware that they are impacting real peoples lives. Providing poor quality work is often damaging. Think of it in terms of a plumber working in your kitchen. If the plumber is lazy, uses the wrong size fitting, does not use the correct kind of pipe and then leaves you to deal with the water damage, is this appropriate? No! So be sure to drill your skills.

SEARCHING THE WATERS OF THE BODY
If you are a visual you can also search the waters of the body which store memory to gain information. Ask for permission before using this form of information access as doing a read

on an individual without their permission can be perceived by that individual as a violation of their space.

Once you have permission, you will once again begin with ground, center and align your heart. Then define the question which the parishioner/client wants answered as precisely as possible. Charge the question and send it and a single pulse to the person's field. See what lights up. Then charge the individual areas which light up and watch the "movies" of the person's life experience which will display in the field.

Watch each area from dullest (longest in the field and least charged) to brightest. Then spend several minutes thinking through what you have seen and combining the information into a cohesive whole. Remember this is just more information. Once you have the additional information organized then share the specifics of what you have seen with the client/parishioner using the ethical rules in Appendix A as the parameters for what material you share.

SURRENDERING TO THE DIVINE

Once your connection is established there will be times when information will simply come to you. It is often unexpected and not information you necessarily want to have. Be patient with yourself in those instances. There will generally be a good reason for why you will have received the information. If you are patient, the reason will come to light and you will be happy to have the information. At the same time, if you are receiving information out of context in quantities which are debilitating you have the right and obligation to say "stop." Send the stop up your established connection to the light of truth and until you say yes to receiving information again the flow will generally stop. If it does not check and see if you are properly disconnecting at the end of a session. You do not want to leave the connection in place 24-7. You want to connect, get the necessary information and disconnect. We live in a sea of energy and to maintain connection to this level of flow becomes overwhelming.

To properly disconnect, ground, center, align and pull all extended currents back into the self. Then take three cleansing breaths and deliberately change your minds focus to something mundane like doing laundry or car pools or getting out a newsletter.

Rolling Forward or Backward in time

Another method of accessing information useful to your parishioner/client is to move forward or backward in time. This takes specific training in forward projection or regression. It is not to be done lightly and not to be done without correct training as it often uncovers significant issues. It should only be done when the parishioner/client has the correct psychological support system. While it can provide useful information, anything involving memory is suspect and can be manipulated.

Generally, it is wise to send the parishioner/client for help in this area with someone who is correctly trained to do this type of work. Referral to a trained therapist or hypnotherapist is usually a good choice if progression or regression work is necessary to support a parishioner/client properly.

Connecting to core

One of the methods of accessing information and for moving a parishioner/client into a deeper connection with themselves is to "access core." This is an esoteric technique which has been around for about 6000 years. To begin this process start with grounding, centering and aligning. Then breathe into the belly. Shift your consciousness into the center of the center of the belly and breath. Begin to watch with the mind's eye and look for a spark to flash in the center of the center of the belly (lower tien tien).

When you "see" the spark breath into the spark. You are essentially adding oxygen to the flame. Breathing into the spark, grow it until the charged area fills the belly. Then acting as a tuning fork, brush the edges of your field on the outside edges of the parishioners/clients field. Allow the resonating pattern of the charged field of your core, to vibrate across the field connections and watch as the core in the parishioner/client lifts to match. Coach the individual as they too breathe into this connection. They will be making a connection to the core of themselves and will have an opportunity to perceive how beautiful they are. From this place of connection, they can ask questions of themselves and seek answers internally.

Often in this process you will have to hold their core lifted with your own core lift. This is very important as it can be hard to see your beauty when you are also looking at perceived wrongness. Maintain your core lift with breath. There is no actual physical contact with the parishioner/client at any time in the process. Practice in lifting your core can be done over a period of a week or so. Once you have identified how to access your core, lift your core. Remain with your core lifted for a period of time, supporting another persons connection to their inner beauty becomes joyous. It is amazing to watch as people find their connection to themselves and begin to see their own inner beauty.

Using the Minds Eye Access

One of the most common ways a natural connection is established to intuitive information is through access to the "minds eye." For this access you must have an awareness of how your brain feels, where you think from inside your head and perceive how information flows into your body and your brain.

Grounding, centering and aligning begins the process. Then three cleansing breaths to begin the process of internal focus. Feel where you think from as a perceptive process from inside the self. Is it in the center of the head? Is it to one side of the head? How does it feel to think from the back of the head verses the front of the head? How does it feel to think from the bottom of the head verses the top? Once you have perceived the differences in how you think based on where you think for inside your own head, move the thought into the center of the head. Breathe and be.

Now move to the observer self. As you watch what happens notice where the information enters/appears inside your head. Ask yourself a question and watch where the answer comes. Think about an image which you have seen in a movie and watch where the image comes into your brain. Allow a memory of something to come and notice how the images related to that memory enter the brain. Each of these is an image pathway. Practice these steps until you can distinguish each of these separate pathways so that you know what kind of information you are getting.

Now focus in particular on the pathway where you ask a question and receive images. Note that spot in particular. When you receive intuitive information it is most likely to enter through this "mind's eye" pathway. Again there is no substitute for drill. This is a skill. Spend 10 minutes each day for two weeks practicing connecting to this minds eye. Ask specific question about your own life and see what kind of information you receive. Remember there is no need to fear, if you do not like the information you receive you can change the situation to something more satisfying.

Over the course of the two weeks make note of your questions, impressions, information and when you need to change situations. This will help you develop a road map for your own future.

CHAPTER FIVE

Interpretation of Information

A challenge for all those who share intuitive information is the accuracy in the interpretation of that information. It is important to be accessing the information if at all possible while holding the light of truth. It improves accuracy. If you are unable to hold the light of truth for whatever reason, observe carefully how you are accessing the information and in what form the information is arriving.

For example: If information is coming in the form of memories, it may mean that only one element is relevant to what the parishioner/client is experiencing or the individual may be having a similar experience to the practitioner. It is wise in that situation to question the person more fully around issues relevant to the memory being presented. For example: whenever I see my fathers face when I am getting information I have learned over the years that it is my unconscious sharing the parishioner/client has daddy stuff which is relevant.

If for example the information is coming in direct images, through your image access point in your head then the images being presented are likely more literal. You would then share the specific images themselves with color, texture, size etc as exactly as possible. If the information is coming in a sensate way, your leg is aching, or your toes feel crushed, you might discuss with the person the physical circumstances around which their issue revolves. If the information is coming as a taste or smell, stating exactly what you get without elaboration or interpretation is key. If you know your unconscious generally uses a particular taste or smell to have a specific meaning keep that in mind and check for relevance.

One day I was working with an individual and kept hearing a particular song in my head. I shared the lyrics with the person without interpretation and they began to cry. The client's father had recently passed away and the last thing that they had done together was attend a concert and decide that this was the best song of the concert. The client then made a connection to their father and was able to mourn when they had not been able to do so.

So share information specifically. Be as accurate as possible. Do not embellish or interpret. And pay attention to how, what type and where you are accessing the information inside your own head.

THE EGO SELF
AND THE NEEDS OF THE UNCONSCIOUS

You will also want to discover if and when the information you are getting is noise. Noise is not unusual when accessing intuitive information.

Noise happens in several different ways:
1. As you start to access intuitive information if there is noise on the wave/signal that you are trying to access then you may get images that have nothing to do with the

information you are trying to access. You can recognize this situation from a buzzing sound as you access the information, or a series of images that are random in nature and feel far removed from the information you are seeking, they will feel disconnected and distant or the images will make you feel as if you need to gag. In this situation say to yourself, "this is noise and it is not in truth." Then deliberately align yourself with the light of truth and flow light into the wave to clear the noise off of it.

2. Noise on the wave may happen when you deny correct information. Your unconscious will then try to send you signals that you have liked in the past to satisfy you. When you get a series of images that you have seen in the past that have been correct, go back to the image that you received first. Then breathe and allow that image to come back in. Do not interpret. Simply see what is there.

3. Noise may happen when you try to superimpose interpretations on the information as it is coming in. Be aware as you receive information you need to be passive, receptive and deliberately stop the brain from deciding what the information means. Instead simply see what comes in.

Noise can also happen when our ego is engaged in the process of sharing information. One of the questions that it is wise to explore is "why do this work?" Are you engaged in this process to serve others or to have them love you so that you feel validated and valued as a person? This work can be validating but it is first and foremost an act of service. Do keep that in mind as you work with parishioners/clients.

Are you aware as a practitioner of why you are engaging in this work? Have you spent time focusing on your reasons so that you understand what has brought you to this pathway? Is it altruism or the need to control someone else? Is it compassion for another or the need to acquire love for yourself? Is it joy in the sharing or the need to be right? Is it gratitude for the connection to all of the grace and majesty that is this amazing world we live in or the need to just feel a connection to someone, anyone?

Spend some time and explore these questions in detail. Once you have discerned your reasons be sure to nurture yourself outside of the parishioner/client contact in the ways that you need and that are satisfying. It is not your parishioners/clients job to make you feel good about yourself.

What is your unconscious vocabulary

As we have discussed, each person is a work of art. Each person, even twins, have separate and unique experiences. Because each person's experiences are unique, the way, images, sounds, tastes etc in which they receive intuitive information will be unique. One of the challenges you will face is that you must learn the language of your own unconscious and intuitive process. There is no alternative since your unconscious is unique to you. In this it must be you who discover the specifics. And it is a process.

Keep a log of meanings of images, tastes, smells, colors, sense of heat or cold etc. Over time you will see patterns in the type of image/taste/smell/sound which you can identify with greater specificity. As you begin to identify the meaning of the information being provided by your intuition, your unconscious etc, your sense of satisfaction in your own reliability will also reinforce the accuracy of your connection. The specificity and accuracy of information will continue to improve over time but you must pay attention to the meanings to have the process be reinforced appropriately.

Keep in mind when you deny the information which is coming in initially, the unconscious will try to supply what it thinks you want instead. So it will share many of the successful pieces of information you received and correctly identified and felt satisfaction about in the past. You will need to ask yourself the question - "is my unconscious sharing information that has been successful in the past so it gives me what it thinks I want (this is a kind of noise!) or am I accessing real information?"

Be very sure to check the pathway which is being used to access the information when you deny initial input. And be sure when the session is over to review the information you dismissed so that you can be sure why you dismissed it. It is not unusual for information which is being dismissed to be accurate when viewed from a larger perspective once the aspect of noise has been eliminated. Also notice if it is one specific type of information that you regularly deny as being correct. Any practitioner can develop a level of compassion fatigue that diminishes their accuracy. If you find that you are regularly dismissing information about car accidents or famine, or rape or illness pay attention. The next time you get such images you may find that you need to pay attention instead of dismissing the information.

SEPARATION OF THE NEEDS OF THE SELF FROM THE NEED TO SERVICE THE LONGING OF THE OTHER

One of the challenges that a practitioner may face is the need to make someone who is in distress for whatever reason, happier or feel better. If a parishioner/client is coming to you for support, it is wiser long term to share information accurately than to share information that just makes the person feel good. Feelings are often fleeting. Accurate information is useful and may help the individual make a change which has long lasting and very positive effects.

ARE YOU STEREO-TYPING OR LOOKING AT CATEGORIES OF BEHAVIOR

Another area which catches unsuspecting practitioners is when they generalize behavior based on either physical presence, assumptions based on persona, language usage, or dress. While all of these aspects of the person in front of you are interesting input into the whole of your information, judgments based on these external factors have no place in intuitive and compassionate work.

Let me share some experiences to illustrate this rational.
1. I was working with a client for the first time and the client came in with a tear in the shoulder of their shirt. I could have assumed any of the following:
    - That the client was making a fashion statement.
    - That the client was impoverished.

- That the client had mental health issues and felt comfortable only in that shirt.
- That the client was playing the cool persona.

The client had actually been in a car accident the night before. They had come directly from the hospital where they had sat beside their spouse who was in difficulty. They had called and scheduled that morning specifically to get information to help the person in the hospital.

2. A client brought in a cousin as a gift for a session. The new client spoke as if they were a country person. I could have assumed the following:
   - That the person had limited language skills.
   - That the person was not as intellectual as some people seem to be.
   - That the person was a blue collar worker or laborer.

The new client was one of the largest land owners in my state. They held two advanced degrees but they had been up for two days with some sick livestock and were very tired. As a result of the exhaustion they were speaking more colloquially.

3. A client came in for a session on crutches. They did not want to discuss their physical situation. I could have assumed:
   - That they were suffering from a major illness.
   - That they had a new injury.
   - That they needed some kind of health care support.

The client was an actor who I later found out was practicing getting around on crutches to learn more about the kinds of challenges people who are less mobile face.

Ask questions of your client's. Do not assume. You are not doing a cold psychic reading on a random person you have never seen before. Instead you are acting in support of a parishioner/client and seeking the most complete and truthful answers you can discover.

Are you sharing phony psychobabble?

It is a discipline in which one must engage to be sure that one does not share misinformation simply because it is easier than explaining that you are not getting any particular insights on that particular issue. It is also a discipline in which you must engage to not do pseudo-psychoanalysis. Far too many times, clients have come to a session saying "xyz told me I had cancer." Or "pqr told me that I was bipolar." Or "I was told that this is my problem because my karma is so dark and I must atone for all the killings I have done in past lives." Or "I have been told I am a drama queen which is why I get so upset." Or "I have been told that if I really wanted to get well, I would get well." Or "I have been told that I am not spiritually evolved enough which is why I am not getting well."

This kind of information is deeply damaging to a parishioner/client and is completely out of the scope of practice of someone sharing intuitive information. Here are the general "shalt not's" to keep in mind:

1. You may not give any kind of a medical diagnosis, no matter what images you see, unless you are a licensed medical professional and it is within your scope of practice. Instead you refer to a physician or appropriate allied medical health professional and send a letter about the individual to the practitioner with the information which you have received.

2. You may not give any kind of psychological diagnosis, no matter what images you see, and even if you hear "this person is suffering from (psychological diagnosis)" unless you are a licensed psychological or medical practitioner. Instead you refer to a psychologist and send a letter about the individual to the practitioner with the information which you received.

3. You may not prescribe or recommend vitamins, herbs, or supplements of any kind unless you are a nutritionist or a medical practitioner even if you see exactly what the person should be taking. Instead you refer to a nutritionist and send a letter about the individual to the nutritionist with the information which you have received.

4. You may not recommend specific physical exercises unless it is within your training and scope of practice. Instead you refer to an exercise physiologist or physical therapist and send a letter about the individual to the practitioner with the information which you have received.

5. Do not use a vocabulary which is unsuited to the person in front of you. Try to use words and metaphors that match the vocabulary of the person with whom you are working.

6. Do not use psychological or medical terms even if you are not making a diagnosis. People who come to you for assistance will come from many different backgrounds. While you may have used psychological terms on a regular basis growing up, many people do not. Instead see if you can find more common terms.

Don't interpret!
Say what you saw exactly

It is incredibly important to not interpret information as it comes to you. There cannot be enough stress placed on this. If you interpret information and make assumptions to fit popular phrases you can damage people. When individuals come to you for support and you give them information which is not accurate you also damage yourself, your credibility and your integrity. Always be prepared to instead say "I do not know." Or "I am not getting anything which will help you."

When you give information give precise and correct information. For example you might say "I see a cherry red polo shirt and it is hanging against a white door of some kind." The same kind of thing with interpretation might be "I see clothing hanging up in someone's bed room."

The actual situation was that the shirt was what someone looked up and saw when they found their uncle dead on the floor at the age of 8 and they had blocked the memory. They could not understand why they had panic attacks when ever they were in a room which was painted white.

Another example: You might say "I have an image of a boat that has rusty metal sides. The boat goes above my head. I smell water that has a sour smell. It is daylight and then it is dark." If you had interpreted the information you might say "I see a big metal boat on a river." The actual situation was when the client was 4 and fell into a pond and was drowning. A metal rowboat was close by and pulled them out of the water. It was where their fear of water came from.

So be precise. Share color, shape, size, texture, materials, smells, sounds, etc but do not interpret the information you receive.

CHAPTER SIX

APPROPRIATE SHARING OF INTUITIVE INFORMATION

Beyond learning your personal intuitive vocabulary, it is important to understand how different aspects of daily experience impact life. When you read esoteric literature of many cultures, the factors involved in the creation of all of life's actions and physical manifestations generally have the following aspects noted:

THE APPEARANCE: the external and perceptible forms, or physical aspects of life.

THE NATURE: the spiritual or mental aspects of life.

THE ENTITY: the form that manifests the appearance and nature.

THE POWER: the inherent power or energy of life.

THE INFLUENCE: the action produced when latent energy is activated.

THE INTERNAL CAUSE: the cause latent in life which has a corresponding effect, which can remain dormant.

THE RELATION: the external cause which activates the internal cause.

THE LATENT EFFECT: the effect produced in the depths of life when an internal cause is triggered by an external cause.

THE MANIFEST EFFECT: what actually happens that you can perceive.

THE CONSISTENCY FROM BEGINNING TO END: the perfect integration of these factors into every moment of life.

When one looks at the various individual aspects of a situation additional information which may be relevant to a parishioner/client will appear. It is not unusual for a practitioner to receive information about an individual for much longer than the actual session period. In fact the information may come prior to the session or post session. Be sure to make note of the additional information and be sure to look carefully at the individualized aspects for additional wisdom.

You may want/need to explore the culture of the person you are supporting. Your intuitive aspect will not see the boundaries between cultures and it may share the images that have a direct relationship to that culture. Though it will be in the language of your personal vocabulary the information may need a second level of understanding.

For example if you receive information through traditional Chinese Medicine imagery you may want to translate the information in the following way:

Small Wood – Viscosity of the Wave
Large Wood – Density of the Wave
Small Earth – Consistency of the Wave
Big Earth – Stability the Wave
Metal – Tensile strength of the Wave
Fire – Charge on the Wave
Water – Flow of the Wave
Air – Resonance/Harmonics on the Wave

Being aware of and sensitive to the needs of other cultures is very important and should be actively studied so mistakes that have great impact are not made. For example: I brought fruit to a session and offered it to a client who came for information about a health situation. What I did not know was that in that person's culture, a gift of fruit meant that they were going to die. It was very important when I had this pointed out to me that I called and discussed this with the client so that they were aware that it was simply that I had overflow from one of my fruit trees and that I had seen nothing that said they were going to die.

In Appendix A, there are a series of questions that you need to memorize and ask yourself prior to sharing any intuitive information. These questions have been developed over hundreds of years and it is wise to learn them well as the guidance inherent in the form will help to keep your sharing in a realm where it creates value for both you and your parishioner/client.

WHAT TO DO WHEN YOU GET NOTHING

"Nothing, I'm getting nothing," can be the correct response when you are in fact getting nothing. You will not be able to support each and every person when they come to you. Sometimes it is because it is not the correct time. Sometimes it is because they need to search out the information through a different path. Sometimes, is it because you did not do good self-care and cannot access the information. The underlying reason, while it may be relevant does not change the answer. If you are getting nothing say so. Do not lie. Do not share psychobabble. Do not share when you do not know. Stop and depending on the reason you are not getting information, reschedule for another day.

SUPPORT SYSTEM ASSESSMENT

Before you share information of any kind with a parishioner/client it is important to assess their support system.

You might ask several of the following questions:
1. Are there family members or close friends available for support?

2. If there are family members available, is it a functional family. Do those members in fact have the capacity to support?

3. Does this person have an appropriate outside support system? (Be sure to have a referral list available for your local area.)

4. Does the person have appropriate financial means to get the support they need?

5. Does the person have the appropriate physical means to get the support that they need?

6. What part of these things need to be in place prior to your sharing your intuitive information?

7. How will you support the parishioner/client in getting the support they need? (This should be done with appropriate boundaries.)

8. Once this support system is in place, when will you share your intuitive information.

If the support system is in place then sharing you information in an appropriate manner is not an issue. But it is your responsibility to be sure the person has a support system in place prior to sharing any information which will be challenging for them to hear.

Power and Control

Another challenge is to share information in such a way that you do not make yourself powerful at the expense of the parishioner/client. There is always a power exchange when there is an exchange of information involved.

One may fall into any of these aspects by mistake:
1. If I make myself appear powerful the person will do what I tell them and then their life will get better because of what I told them to do.

2. If I make myself appear powerful then the person will back off, go away and stop questioning me.

3. If I make myself appear powerful lots of people will come and ask me for advice and this will mean I am a good person.

4. If I make myself appear powerful then I will keep myself safe.

5. If I make myself appear powerful then people will love me so then I can love myself.

It is wise not to get caught in the fallacies of power dynamics. In the end everyone is a looser.

Explore the need for power.
In what situations do you feel uncertain?
Why do you experience that uncertainty?
Is that uncertainty appropriate?
When you share information with a parishioner/client what do you gain in power?
What do you loose in power?
What does the parishioner/client gain in power?
What does the parishioner/client lose in power?

In your sharing of information be aware of the power dynamics so that you can mitigate them. In the sharing with a parishioner/client the information needs to be given from a place of neutrality, compassion and wisdom. Not from a place of power. Instead, when you feel the need to share from a place of power choose instead to move into connection with the Divine and be in the light of truth.

Another aspect is of course control. "Hi ho, hi ho, it's all about control!" We explored briefly some aspects of why you became involved in this work. Often among the less altruistic reasons, it is in part to learn about how the world works and to gain some type of control over our environment. It is deeply important to keep a sense of this need if it is actively working in your life.

You cannot manage or rein in this aspect of self without awareness. The need for control comes when we fear. Fear is both a choice and an emotional response to environmental stimuli. When the need for control appears check first, "am I safe?" If you are safe then there is no real reason to respond with fear. Relax, drop the need for control and move back into joy and compassion as a choice.

When one makes the conscious choice to move back into joy and compassion, one begins to transform one's life until the episodes where the fear arises simply do not occur. You also have a choice when you are weaving your life to choose situations in which you are comfortable. You do not need to place yourself in situations which you are unsafe. You have the right to say "no."

OVER SHARING

Over sharing is a common issue when you share with parishioners/clients in the beginning of your supportive practice. It is difficult in the beginning not to share as much information as you get because it is a relief to have the information come through and it is exciting to be able to share something that may provide deep value to the person. Be sure to go back to the list of questions to ask yourself which are listed in Appendix A. Also, keep watch for glazed eyes. Even using the correct boundaries a person can become overwhelmed with the information which they are receiving. It can happen with a single sentence. Many people live in a culture of denial. Often for one who lives in a culture or environment of denial, the truth, even when stated in a fashion which is gentle and kind, is too much. So watch for glazed eyes and be compassionate.

IMPACT OF THE INFORMATION

Repeat three times please, "be gentle, be kind, do they really need this information." Since each and every person who exists is a work of art with special and often subtle gifts to the world, becoming aware of the impact of the information which you have just shared is important. I had a very close call once where I shared some information with a person who then attempted suicide. Their reason for the attempt, "you saw me. That means that I was going to be raped again and I could not take the waiting." The person grew up in an abusive environment and was in a deep personal struggle at the time. Do be sure to dialogue with your parishioner/client about what the information means to them and how they see the impact on their life. Gently, gently and with wisdom. And refer to support as necessary.

HOW TO SHARE/WEIGHT OF THE WORDS

Words have impact. Words have weight. Always take a beat pause prior to sharing any information. Choose your words so that there is no judgment in them. Choose your words so that they are gentle and kind. If you cannot share the information without judgment: DO NOT SHARE.

Do your own process work, go to supervision or counseling support and get clear first. Wait to share until you can share without judgment. Remember most judgment comes out of fear. Fear is a choice. Choose compassion and truth instead.

Do not reinforce negative information because the situation can change

Always keep in mind that each person has free will. Thus the information which you are sharing today may not be correct tomorrow. The human must live on the edge of chaos in order to survive. We must be able to adapt as our environment changes. If we cannot adapt, if we cannot change then we cannot live. Be sure to share with your parishioner/client that they have the option to choose another path. They have the right to make a fresh or new choice and know that you are there to support them in whatever choice they make.

Information is just that. Intuitive information is just more information. It may bring the gift of new insight or wisdom but in the end it is only important if it is a cause for action, to move us forward into a healthier and more positive way of living.

Do not get caught in parlor games

If you hear yourself stating a "truism," stop, reground, center and align. You are not a "psychic" though there are those that will believe that the sharing of intuitive information makes you a psychic. You are not having grand mystic experiences full of drama and pathos. You are carefully sharing information which comes to you in the light of truth at the specific request of an individual for support.

That the individual has made a specific request is key. Do not volunteer information off the cuff. Do not share information about another person unless you have their express verbal permission. Do not share information unless you are in an appropriate setting where confidentiality can be maintained.

Personal information when shared publicly can be devastating. Never ever share a person's private information in a public setting. It is beyond inappropriate to share their information in public. Instead, if they are in a crisis, find a quiet place to talk or schedule them instead at an appropriate time and in an appropriate setting. It is not that you will not be called on for information in public settings. You will and it will happen often. It is that you manage the setting in which you share that information so that you are always in integrity.

Limits of the Intuitive

While intuitive information may be tremendously valuable to the parishioner/client each person has their own sense of timing on which to act on information. Each person will have their own interpretation of the information which you share. Each person will have their own choices to make based on the information you share.

Don't force your interpretation on someone else

Be careful to share information with precision as encouraged with the limit that you do not force any particular interpretation on to the parishioner/client. To force an interpretation is a power aspect. Instead choose compassion, accuracy, state only what information you have and let the person interpret in the way in which the information is correct for them. Do discover how they are seeing the information. Do discover whether or not they feel the information has anything in particular to share with them that is relevant to their life. Do not interpret.

DO NOT DECIDE ANYTHING FOR THE INDIVIDUAL

It can be an easy choice to guide someone into the path we feel is correct for their life. It is also a poor choice. The individual who is receiving the information needs to make the choices for their own life, free of coercion and judgment. It is a sacred act to support someone in their life journey. Do not take away their opportunity to create their life in the way in which is correct for them. Instead witness the beauty of the act of the creation of someone's life and support them as they develop the life which will be fulfilling to them.

DO NOT REMOVE THE INDIVIDUALS OPPORTUNITY FOR TRANSFORMATION

It can be both tremendously difficult to watch someone you care about make what you feel is the wrong choice for their life and tremendously painful. When and if you find yourself in this type of situation remind yourself that people are works of art and if given the correct support evolve in their own time and space into the amazing and sacred being they are becoming. Keep your opinions to yourself as they are based on your own life and your own work of art. Allow instead the grace and space for the other person to create their work of art in the way that is correct for them. There will be time when a parishioner/client will use the information you have provided in a way that you discern is less than optimum. Allow them the space for learning and transformation. It is often life's most challenging lessons which bring us the most wisdom when we look back on them. Give the gift of space to learn and transform and witness the beauty and wisdom which can be created when we walk beside someone in a place of compassion, truth and grace and not of judgment.

CHAPTER SEVEN

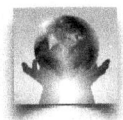

INSIDE AND OUTSIDE THE SELF

The skills building which allows for the development of appropriate boundaries, accurate intuitive information and the separation of emotional noise is not simple. It takes time. It takes drill. It takes discipline. You are working with another being and that act is sacred. You have a deep responsibility to support that individual to the best of your ability. So do not fail yourself. Do the drill. Develop solid skills.

GENETICS AND EPIGENETICS:
LIMITS OF TRANSFORMATION

No one can tell you how much you may or may not transform. No one can tell your parishioners/clients how much they may transform. We just do not have that kind of knowledge yet. Our science is showing us that even the genetic code, which thirty years ago was thought to be carved in stone, today is recognized as being able to make active changes. So as you provide information, be sure that you do not set limits on your own skills. Something which can be challenging at the beginning of a process with practice becomes effortless. It takes many years to make a great skier, dancer, basket ball player etc. Years of practice which include many, many hours of drill. Give yourself the gift of time and drill your skills. Learn your craft so that you are confident that your information is provided carefully and well.

GAINED AND LOST OPPORTUNITIES

When one presents opportunities for change and transformation to another, there are possibilities for things gained and lost in the process of transformation. If the opportunity arises to discuss the potential gains and losses that change creates in a mater of fact way it is all to the good. Change can be difficult for many people and if some of the options are made clear and the ramifications of the changes are made clear, this allows a person to make a more fully informed choice.

This process is different than making a choice for someone else or telling them what you think their best choices are going to be. Instead, this is a discussion of the many options that can be created by change. Have the person with whom you are working share what they think will be the options that might be created in the process of making changes. When you discuss these things in advance, it makes the path of the change clearer, less scary and more easily accessed.

FEAR AS A CHOICE

As discussed at several points in this book, fear is a choice. Excitation of the neurological system releases adrenalin as a physiological response to both excitement and fear. The body does not distinguish between excitement and fear. It is exactly the same process. You as an individual determine how to evaluate the body's reaction to stimulation. So you may choose excitement, adventure, opportunity. Or you may choose fear.

Choose wisely for yourself and for the person you are supporting. Share this information with the person you are supporting so that they also understand that fear is a choice.

Fear of Being Noticed

Being different in our society is not easy or simple. Being intuitive and sharing information which you directly identify as being intuitive information may be difficult or create an awkward response between you and the person you are attempting to help. If you personally have difficulty with being noticed you may want to share your insights in such a way that they are suggestions or options for paths to follow. Though you share the information as suggestions, be sure to remain in truth.

The same obligations for integrity remain. Be sure to work on your fear to clear it and to choose an option which is healthier for you. You will want to move forward without fear as you progress over time. Most people who share intuitive information on a regular basis discover that when they no longer fear sharing the information clearly and designate it as intuitive information, issues which parishioners/clients have with the type of sharing go away.

Techniques of down regulation and forgiveness

Many pieces of information which are brought forward through intuition create a significant emotional response in the listener. These reactions may include sobbing, yelling, foul language, breaking things and becoming violent. If your listener has a significant response to the information, do not simply turn them loose to leave and drop them emotionally.

You have a duty to share ways to manage the challenges brought forth by a significant emotional response. Further, you have a duty to share referral information which will help them handle the emotional response which they are experiencing. Teach them correct breathing. Teach them to ground, center and align. Teach them to shift to a happy or neutral thought. Teach them to forgive themselves and others.

Choosing Joy and Happiness

One of the things which you can practice which will then spill over into your intuitive information is to consciously choose joy and happiness whenever possible. For example: you are at an airport and all of the planes are grounded. You are exhausted. You could choose to be aggressive with the hotel staff from whom you are trying to get a local room for the night or you could choose to be joyous that you are not out in the weather and that you have sufficient funds to get a hotel room for the night.

When you take advantage of the opportunity to recognize a gift and receive that gift joyfully you strengthen the presence joy has in your life. This in turn strengthens the presence joy will have in the intuitive information which you share and the way in which your parishioners/clients receive and act on the intuitive information.

Being different in a good way

Intuitive skills come from hunter-gatherer skills. They have allowed us to find the herd in the forest so that we may feed our family. It is that sense of how things work and need to be. Allowing yourself to move into that traditional connection of knowing and providing lets you be different from others but in a good way. It lets you bring truth to those who are seeking. It lets you bring wisdom and experience to those who need information.

It lets you support the creation of a better and more joyous world filled with grace and compassion. Allow yourself to be different in a way that supports your community and creates wisdom.

CHAPTER EIGHT

FINAL WORDS

In the process of working through the various techniques, aspects and pieces of information which are discussed in this book, one hopes that progress has been made in establishing, developing and deepening individual and personal connection to intuition and distinguishing it from emotional response. I would encourage each of you to listen to the internal self-voice and be strict in the area of sharing only what is really necessary and in truth with those that come to you for help.

Act always from a place of compassion. Act always in the best interests of the person to the highest and best ability that you have at the time. Keep yourself as clear as possible for the act of sharing this kind of information is a sacred trust and must not be abused.

Notice if you really, really, really, need to share a piece of information and if you do stop. Recognize that you are not clear when there is that much internal pressure to share information. Recognize that having access to more information does not make you a better person than the person who comes to you for help. It just makes you a person with more information. Instead it is the meticulous integrity with which you share the information that supports your growth as a person.

Do not fall into the trap of power and control. Do not fall into the trap of telling others how to run their lives for this denies them the opportunity to create their own life. Rather use the information and insight to guide the person to what will be the most fulfilling experiences for them and for their life. Support their ability to take advantage of the opportunity for change and growth.

Come from the heart, hold appropriate boundaries, and support joy and compassion. May Grace be yours in all that you do.

APPENDIX A.

Ethics of Sharing

The ethical sharing of information with clients and parishioners is critical. Not all people will have the support systems necessary to be able to hear and receive the information a practitioner receives. In addition, not all people will have a personal paradigm that makes them comfortable receiving this type of information. Always be careful and respectful of the person in your sharing. Sharing information in a way that creates a power dynamic with the person is to be avoided. Remember that no medical or psychological diagnosis may be made at any time unless the practitioner has that training and skill within their legally defined scope of practice.

Steps to take to assess if the information is correct and to be shared:

Is it true?
If you are not sure then work from the position that it is not true and do not share the information until you are sure.

Have you verified it with more than one sense?
Be sure that you can verify the information with more than one sense.

CAN ANOTHER PERSON VERIFY YOUR IMPRESSIONS?
Get another opinion especially if you may not be clean in this area.

IS IT KIND?
If it is not do not tell them.

DOES THE PERSON NEED TO KNOW THE INFORMATION?
If they do not need to know this information do not share it. If they do need to know the information share it with discernment.

WHAT WILL YOU GAIN BY SHARING THE INFORMATION?
Be very clear. You owe it to yourself not to create negative karma.

WHAT WILL THE PERSON GAIN BY RECEIVING THE INFORMATION?
Run possibilities in your head. Expect the unexpected.

CAN YOU GIFT THE INFORMATION TO THE PERSON IN SUCH A WAY THAT YOU SAY THE WORDS WITHOUT BLAME AND JUDGMENT?
If you cannot then do not say it until you can. Do your processing at home not in the session. The parishioner/client is not your therapist.

ARE YOU MAKING A MEDICAL DIAGNOSIS?
If so is it within your scope of practice?

DOES THE PERSON HAVE ADEQUATE SUPPORT FOR THE PERIOD THAT THEY ARE PROCESSING THE INFORMATION THAT YOU HAVE PROVIDED TO THEM?

If they do not see that they get support before you share this information with them.

WORKBOOK

CHAPTER NINE

Introduction to Workbook

I hope that my efforts here will aid people of many types. Developing your intuitive skills is critical toward being responsive to the people you are supporting I ask only that all those that read this book, hold this process in integrity and grace as you bring your light to the world. I call on each of you to discipline yourselves. Be courageous but have that be tempered by wisdom. Be supportive but have that be tempered by appropriate boundaries.. It is my hope that all of these parts will be held in grace by individuals who use this book, drill these skills, and support the health and healing of our world.

How To Use This Book

This is a companion workbook to Accessing Truth: Emotion, Intuition and Compassion. It is not intended as a stand alone text. Each of the exercises listed in this book should be practiced until you become competent. This workbook is here to help you drill the material. There is no substitute for drill. Think of how long it takes to make a great base ball player or how long it takes to make a superb pianist. There are many, Many hours of practice. So do the exercises and drill, drill, drill.

Review the rules for sharing in Appendix A.
Then begin the skills drill in Chapter 1. Before you attempt any other skills you must be able to ground center and align. Then drill until your can establish a direct connection for intuitive information. I caution you to be sure to establish your own channel for information each time you do this work.

There is lots of noise in our environment today. Establishing a clean and clear connection is vital to the development of accurate information. So be sure to deliberately establish your connection to the stream of information each and every time. This will improve your accuracy and build your skills long term until the process is effortless. Once that set of skills is mastered the exercises in the book may be done in any order that feels correct for your personal skills development.

Workbook for Chapter One

What is emotion?

Definition of emotion
Emotion may be defined in medical terms, in humanistic terms and in structured logic. For our purposes we will consider emotion both a feeling state and a response which produces a feeling state which is often strong and which may arise faster than thought. It is often produced as a limbic system response and may include physiological and behavioral changes in the body.

How are your emotions experienced?
Take a moment and pull out a small notebook that you can fit in your pocket. Carry it for the next 24 hours and note down each time you have a significant emotional response. See what kinds you actually have.

So how do you personally experience emotion? Write down your physical sensate experience of several different types of emotional experience. Be as detailed as possible. Include: happy, joyous, sad, angry, frustrated and calm.

Happy:
_____
_____
_____

Joyous:
_____
_____
_____

Sad:
_____
_____
_____

Angry:
_____
_____
_____

Frustrated:
_____
_____
_____

Calm:
_____
_____
_____

What are the predominant ways in which you have emotional experiences?
_____
_____
_____

Would you describe yourself as a calm person? An angry person? A rational person? A sad person? A depressed person? An optimistic person?
_____
_____
_____

Then check in with a few friends.
Ask three or more people to describe what your most common emotional responses are to daily life. How would they describe you?
_____
_____
_____

Then ask one or two family members how would they describe you?
_____
_____
_____

DEFENSIVE PATTERNS

Emotional experiences can cause us to use defensive responses to life situations. These defensive responses can be verbal, physical or may extend into what some people see as the energetic/extended part of human consciousness. These responses may include things like yelling, making a snarky comment, stomping feet, throwing something, brooding, withdrawing, changing body position, shaking etc. When we engage in a defensive response, current physiological theory supports the idea that we are protecting the "self" or the "core part of the persona." Recognition of the type of defensive response in which we are engaged is important.

Once you recognize you have engaged a defensive response you can begin to learn the following:

1. What are your triggers?
_____
_____
_____

2. Why did you feel the need to trigger?
_____
_____
_____

3. Should you have triggered or is this an automatic or "left-over from another situation" response?
_____
_____
_____

4. Is your emotional or physical response bigger than the situation really calls for?

_____
_____
_____

5. How might you interrupt your defensive response in the future?

_____
_____
_____

6. What new choice of behavior are you going to make when you recognize that you have triggered and you are in defense?

_____
_____
_____

7. How will you implement that choice in daily life?

_____
_____
_____

These are some of the interventions you can use to interrupt your personal defensive responses:
1. Ground, center and align. This interrupts the defensive response.
2. Breathe and switch your focus to a different thought.
3. Breathe in the word "grace" and breathe out the word "compassion."

4. Do a remembering moment where you deliberately remember a joyous experience or an experience when you felt gratitude.
5. Send the energy of the defensive response into the ground. Let it drain out of the body.

Now see if you can create several other interventions which you might use to interrupt your patterned responses. Be sure to write them down.

Intervention 1:
_____
_____
_____

Intervention 2:
_____
_____
_____

HEALING THROUGH EMOTIONAL EXPRESSION

There appear to be a number of different ways in which emotions may be experienced and possibly be cleared:

Dialogue, listening, an act of creation such as writing music or a book,   participating in sports, climbing a mountain, setting a goal for the self and achieving it, and experiencing nature are all among the possibilities.

Look for an emotional experience that is in excess of what would be considered an appropriate level of response for the situation. Then try one of the methods listed like writing a book or in a journal, going on a serious hike or watching a sunset and see what your response is to the action. write directly about your experience. Be as honest and complete as you are able to be.

_____
_____
_____
_____
_____
_____

Take a moment now and make a list of ways that you have cleared an emotional response in the past.

_____
_____
_____
_____
_____

GROUNDING AS THE START

There are many different ways to engage in what is popularly and esoterically called "Grounding." In grounding through visualization, breath, directed thought, meditation, sports exercise, or dance (to name a few of the options) one engages to link the physical body to the 7 Hz current which is naturally produced by the Earth.

The hope in "grounding" is to move the body into a receptive state where the current which flows freely over the surface of the Earth also flows freely into and over the body. Keep in mind that many people have a physical, sensate response to the processes listed below.

Below are several methods for accessing this "grounding" body feeling. Practice one or all of these at least ten min twice a day for the next six weeks:

METHOD 1:
This is a basic method of grounding and may be used by anyone who wishes.

1. Breathe in for a count of 4 and out for a count of 4 three times.
2. Feel your feet on the floor. Are they warm or cold?
3. Allow your feet to feel heavy and solid against the floor.
4. Then using your breath to let go of your feet allow the image of your feet falling through the ground all the way on to the surface of the iron core at the center of the Earth.

5. Allow the warmth of that connection to slide over the surface of the skin and sink into all the cells of the body as that warmth moves up the body.

Method 2:

This is a second basic method of grounding where you align yourself to the perceived consciousness of the Earth.

1. Allow yourself to recognize how you are breathing.
2. Let the breath become gentle and relaxed.
3. Using visualization as a tool to guide body response, see the legs becoming heavy and falling into the Earth.
4. See them slide into the center of the core of the Earth.
5. Breathe and reach out your consciousness much as if you were reaching out your hand to touch the shoulder of a friend and touch the consciousness of the Earth.
6. Allow yourself to receive the current which is gifted to you from this contact with the earth into your physical feet.
7. Let this earth current sink into the tissues of the body.

Method 3:

This is a heart-centered method which still grounds through the base of the field.

1. Breathe and become aware of your heart beating in your chest.

2. Take a second gentle breath and see if you can feel your heart actually beat.
3. Then with the next breath follow the breath into the lungs.
4. Then with the next breath follow the breath all the way into the heart.
5. Then feel a current from the heart traveling down the body and into the legs and from there into the feet.
6. Now follow that current down into the Earth, all the way to the core of the earth, breathing into your heart and into the heart of the earth.
7. Become aware of the consciousness of the Earth, and give a gift of gratitude of your heart light to the Earth as a thank you for the cherishing of your body and your life.
8. Then receive the corresponding gift back along the heart current and into your physical feet and upwards throughout the body tissue.
9. Allow any excess charge to spill out of the head and back down into the core of the earth, once again honoring the earth.

Method 4:

This is an esoteric method of grounding where you anchor the physical form in time and space to 4 directions. This is reported to allow individuals to move forward and backward in time with greater reliability and security.

1. Using imagination as a tool to guide the process, see your feet falling into the core of the earth, then sink the base of your body corona (the charged field which wraps around your body) into the Earth.

2. Reach up from the core into the center point in the center of the belly/tien tien and move a current of the Earth current up through the heart and then up through the top of the head to the point of individuation and into a connection with the Divine.
3. Then sink a tendril of light from the sun to the front of the heart.
4. Then sink a tendril of light from the moon to the back of the heart.
5. Allow the currents of light to move in each direction so that you have twisted all of the strands together and they move up and down the mid-line power current of the body.
6. Allow any excess current to fountain out of the top of the head and flow over the surface of the body back into the earth, so that you are standing as a virtual link between heaven and Earth.

Practice each method of grounding three times. Which one do you feel most comfortable using and why is it comfortable?

_____
_____
_____
_____
_____

Now go out and do things like grocery shopping, laundry, go to the library, go to a sports event, go take a walk in the woods. At each thing practice your grounding. Which one of the methods works best in that kind of environment?

List the environment and they type of grounding that worked best below:

_____
_____
_____
_____
_____
_____
_____
_____

DRAINING EXCESS EMOTION

Excess emotion, an emotional response which is bigger than the situation warrants, is rarely useful. Taking and having control of that excess emotion is an important step in the process of developing body awareness and body management. It is important to distinguish the fact that excess emotional current is different than grounded current. The spectrographic map of various hormones ranges upwards from 20 Hz. Again, grounded current is 6.8 to 7 Hz. You are literally responding to a different range of frequencies. Because current moves faster at higher frequencies it can cancel out or overwhelm your perception of waves that are running at lower rates. So in addition to grounding, learning how to drain off emotional over charge may be a valuable process to learn.

For the next six weeks practice draining off any emotional overcharge that you experience. Try one of the methods listed below:

METHOD 1:

This is a basic method of reducing overcharge in an emotional response by using breath.

1. If you begin to feel fear, rage sorrow or any excess emotion, shift your focus to your breath.
2. Feel the breath entering the body.
3. Feel the air flow down your nose, your throat and into the lungs.
4. Feel the lungs fill.
5. Allow the body to relax as your exhale.
6. 6Bring your mind back to feeling the breath each time it drifts in its focus.
7. Repeat.

METHOD 2:

Excess emotion often happens faster than thought. This is a method of training your body to have an automatic response to excess emotion and draining it off so the physical and verbal actions that follow the experience can be more controlled. This method is particularly useful for people who have raised teenagers!

1. Begin with the breath. Now exhale and try to clear out the breath fully. This will require a little extra push from your belly. Kind of like a grunt.
2. Then just as you would when a teenager comes home at midnight instead of the agreed upon 10pm, let your body move into the form where you "put your foot down."
3. Then release and let the excess emotion drain right out of the body into the ground.

METHOD 3:

In an emergency, excess emotion can often be converted into charge which can be used to help and not harm. If the body perceives something as an emergency when it is not, then that charge needs to be converted another way. This method uses the gathering action of getting ready to make a response as a mechanism toward giving the self a moment of time to think and then make a choice for what you wish to do with the charged you have created. This method is important to drill in non-essential situations so that a body habit pattern becomes engaged and can be used.

1. Perceive when the body is gathering charge.
2. Locate where the charge is occurring in the body.
3. Make a conscious choice where you want to send the energy so that you do not harm anyone including yourself.
4. Take a belly breath and with the exhale send the energy in the direction you have chosen.
5. Repeat until the full charge is released.
6. Consciously relax the muscles/body in the area that charged originally.
7. Breathe into the belly and exhale slowly three times to fully clear.

When you finish your six weeks of practice draining off excess emotion, take a few minutes and write a paragraph or two about your experiences with the process. Include any reminders to yourself that you think you will need in the future.

_____

_____

_____
_____
_____
_____
_____
_____
_____
_____
_____
_____
_____
_____
_____
_____
_____
_____
_____

CENTERING AND ALIGNING

Centering and aligning are the next steps in a complete grounding process. They allow you to move back into truth using visualization and body sensing. Doing both of the exercises below, at least once a day, allows the body to maintain a level of connectedness and allows the self to be more connected to the truth of who you are as an individual. It can also be used anytime one is being swayed by both positive or negative experiences. Remember that all these exercises are focused on helping you to access truth throughout your day no matter that current "life moment" circumstance.

Once you feel as if you have begun to experience grounding as a physical sensate experience begin to practice centering and aligning in your 10 min two times per day practice. Try the methods listed below:

CENTER:
1. Bring Earth energy through feet, legs, pelvis, torso, heart, up to shoulders, then let it flow down arms and hands and at the same time up through neck and head. Then let it flow out through top of head and fountain/cascade down over body to Mother Earth. This creates a rinsing away process to clear the body. Let the excess charge, flow down to Mother Earth and give the noise that has rinsed out of the body as a gift to her so that she can experience what you have experienced.
2. Connect to your heart.
3. Feel the energy moving up and down the midline power current.

ALIGN:
1. Connect to the center of the self and the truth of your existence. Use statements that are truthful like "my address is ...", "my given name is...", or other factual statements.
2. Align your body with that truth.

Practice centering and aligning each time you ground over the next three days. How does centering and aligning change your experience of grounding each day?

1._____

2._____

3._____

LET THE HEART OPEN

Deliberately opening the heart when you receive information is just good manners. It is a way to say "thank you." Always remember that when individuals come to you for insight, the information which you share with them has weight and potentially power. It must be shared accurately, with wisdom and with discernment. Having the heart open as you share allows you to better discern how the information is being received so that you may impart information with great appreciation and consideration of the individual in front of you.

Once you feel that you have gotten the hang of grounding, centering and aligning practice opening the heart each time you do your grounding.

Then begin to practice opening the heart each time you listen to another person. How does listening with an open heart change the way in which you perceive information? List three ways that this process changes how you listen.

1._____

2._____

3._____

FINAL EXERCISE FOR CHAPTER 1 WORKBOOK:
Use this page to write down the key experiences that you have had as you learned to ground, center, align, open your heart and drain any emotional overcharge that you have experienced. Try to include things that you think will be among the most important stories to share with your future parishioner's/client's/student's.

Workbook for Chapter Two

What is Intuition?

Definition of intuition

Intuition can be defined as an instinctive response rather than more conscious and direct forms of thinking or reasoning. It often appears to be an immediate response and can include a sort of all encompassing or total knowing type experience.

How does intuition present itself

Intuitive information comes in many different ways. It can appear using senses or information pathways which one does not expect.

Write down in your notebook your list of personal vocabulary equivalents. For example: if you get an intuitive flash with an image of your father in your personal vocabulary it may mean that the person is dealing with "daddy" stuff. Another example: might be hearing a jingle from a commercial.

A specific phrase from that jingle might have meaning in the situation. Yet another example: smelling sugar cookies baking - if that is a good memory for you - it might be that the situation you will be addressing is linked to a good memory.

If it is a bad memory for you because you burnt the cookies - it might mean that something is literally going to burn.

_____
_____
_____
_____
_____

How many different ways have you personally experienced an intuitive insight? See if you can add to the list of possible pathways.

Memory, Sound bytes, Smells, Tastes, Floating Images, The Flash, Ah Ha Moment, River of Information, Direct Knowing and Minds Eye:

_____
_____

MEMORY

The intuitive and the unconscious use memories to share a variety of types of information with the more conscious mind as the linkage to the conscious mind is already physically in place. The types of information generally include the following:
1. Situations of learning which need to be resolved.
2. Information which matches experiences that one has had in the past and that has a key nugget that is relevant to the information which the unconscious is trying to share with the conscious mind.

3. Specific parts of images like color, physical setting or people who are once again involved.
4. A situation which will take place at the same time of year.

What intuitive information your unconscious is trying to communicate takes practice to recognize. For example: when you see images of children playing baseball it could be that the unconscious it trying to communicate "summer play", "a specific baseball game and an experience related to that game", "an experience that happened while watching baseball", or "an interpersonal interaction having to do with sports." Making a list of possible information with a short description of how you felt physically and emotionally will aid you in more rapid recognition of the actual meaning and will also assist in developing your personal vocabulary with your unconscious. There will always be some direct relationship to the informational response you are trying to access.

Take a minute and write down an experience where memory has been a factor in how your received intuitive information. Be as specific as possible.

_____
_____
_____
_____
_____
_____
_____

Sound bytes

Sound, in particular alert/emergency sounds and pieces of songs are common methods with which intuitive information is communicated. For example: my bank recently closed it's local branch. I needed a new bank that met my specific requirements. I looked at a number of banks in the local area but was not finding what I wanted. Then as I was driving past a shopping center in the local area I heard a jingle I had sung for a commercial. "... that's my bank" was the lyric which played in my head. I did not know there was a bank in that shopping center. I drove in, found the bank, got information on the bank and it was indeed what I was looking for.

Another example: Every time I would walk past an electrical switch in my kitchen I would hear a snapping sound. It made no sense. The lights worked fine. Then one day we had a short because I was running too many things in the kitchen at once. I got an electrician out to upgrade and correct things and as an after thought I asked him to look at the light switch. It turned out that it was an electrical short that was triggering my intuition into making that snapping sound in my head. It was a fire waiting to happen.

Make a list over the course of a week of each of the pieces of songs, commercial jingles, whistles, snaps etc which you hear in your head as part of your daily life and see if they relate in any way to what was happening in your life at the time.

_____

_____

_____

_____
_____
_____
_____
_____
_____
_____
_____

SMELLS

Smells are one of the oldest and strongest senses that we have as humans. When you receive a specific smell in the process of seeking intuitive information pay close attention to it. Again, pay attention to the context. Has the smell come as part of an image? Has the smell occurred spontaneously as you are doing a daily task? Has the smell happened when you are around a specific place which does not fit the environment?

Make a list of smells that have no reason to be in a particular place or associated with a particular situation which you perceive over the course of a week.
List the environment and what you were thinking about at the time.
How does this information enrich the vocabulary list you are creating?
What kind of additional information does it give you?
Do some careful thinking about the specific situations in which the information came to you.
See if you can notice similar situations over the next month. Are you getting information in those similar situations?

If so, be sure to develop a habit of checking in with your sense of smell to see what information it may give you.

_____
_____
_____
_____
_____
_____
_____
_____

TASTES

Like smell, taste is one of our oldest senses. Despite the standard limits of sweet, sour, bitter and salty of our taste buds, extended sensing can give you many more specifics within the context of taste. When having intuitive experiences there are common reports of things like "the taste of dust" linked to historic imagery. Tastes of gun powder, metal and mud have been linked to battles. Tastes of sugar or sweet tastes are often linked to celebrations. The taste of particular foods are often linked to memories which will have elements of significance and relevance to the individual requesting knowledge.

Make a list over the course of a week of all of the times where you get information through taste. How did the information help you? Was the information specific or more general?

_____
_____

FLOATING IMAGES

Become aware of the timing of floating images. When do they happen? Is it at the beginning of more complete information sharing or at the end? Is the information complex or does it just hang in space without a context?

Write down an experience which you have had with floating images. Be sure to list any information you want to have for the future. Include information about time, duration, type of imagery etc.

_____
_____
_____
_____
_____

THE FLASH

An intuitive "flash" or "hit" is among the most common ways in which people sense information. This form of information sharing through the unconscious is usually both specific in one or more details/elements presented and is complete in the information which it is trying to impart. This type of information sharing comes in a fraction of a second.

Write down an experience of "the flash." Include any information that you think will be important for you to know in the future.

_____
_____
_____
_____
_____

It is important to carry a small notebook with which to make notes on experiences such as this type in the beginning of intuitive development and practice, as it will help the intuitive to strengthen the pathways through which accurate and complete information is distributed.

The Aha moment

Intuitive information which comes as insight into how our life experience unfolds and the meaning which our life holds, provides us a way to move forward with our life from a place of greater enrichment and compassion. The *Ah Ha* moment in which we receive this type of information supports our development as a person. It is information which is valuable to us personally and in general is not as relevant to our parishioners/clients. It is a complete information insight which we are meant to put into practice in our daily lives.

Take some time over a period of a week and see if you have any moments that provide you insight into how to better live your life. Note each of these down. Spend ten minutes thinking about each episode and determine if there are actions you can take to make your life work better as a result of these *AhHa* moments. Do all of these moments follow a particular theme? Do all of these moments come with information which will help you to change ingrained behaviors? Do any or all of these moments show you methods of organizing your life to greater effect?

_____
_____
_____
_____
_____
_____
_____
_____
_____

RIVER OF INFORMATION

Share an experience with a friend of information you have received which came in a flow. It does not have to be about them at this time. Use this practice experience to work on how to share information which you receive. Be as specific as possible. Work on descriptions and accuracy with your friend.

A COMPLETE FORM OR DIRECT KNOWING

Similar to the flash experience, an experience of direct knowing comes as a single unit of experience and contains all of the necessary information at one time. The difference is in the way the information comes. Rather than a flash of intuition and perception which is "seen" by the individual, it is information which comes in a direct channel from the Divine. It enters this dimension and frequency range through a connection point between individuated incarnation and the larger all at the edge of the tenth layer of the biofield. The information flows down the midline power current of the body and seats in the brain area first and over a period of a few seconds expands to take in the whole of the body. Where the "flash" experience is the unconscious putting together relevant information combined with unconscious information and perception the "direct knowing" experience comes from outside the individuated incarnation.

Write down an experience you have had in the past of direct knowing. How is it different from the other forms of intuitive insight and information flow? How did the direct knowing aid you? How did the experience affect your perception of the situation to which it was related?

_____
_____
_____
_____
_____
_____
_____
_____

Moments of disorientation or disconnection

When you are seeking intuitive information and you have moments of disorientation or disconnection which either interrupts or happens slightly before the information arrives, ground, ground and reground. This reaction is usually as a result of something in the images being acutely stressful to see.

It may be a disconnection in the belief system of the practitioner who is receiving the information or it may simply be images too painful or horrific to want to see. It can be difficult to see one starvation after the next war after the next murder after the next agony. Remember to be patient with yourself. Ground, center, align and hold compassion for yourself and if you were seeking information for another, hold grace and compassion for them as well.

If the experience of disorientation happens on a regular basis, this is not imagery causing an issue but instead something physiological which needs to be properly explored and addressed. Keep in mind that while this work is both controversial and complex, it needs to be grounded in daily activities that are solidly realistic.

A continuous process of testing the truth of your experiences and the accuracy of your experiences is necessary. Without a commitment to the groundedness of daily life, the demand for internal truth and the continuous development of the skills, it is unwise to follow this path, as more negatives could be created in one's life than value created from it.

There is spiritual value in doing laundry, feeding the dog, scrubbing the floor, and making a good meal when consciousness is brought to the process and love is shared in every interaction. These things keep the balance of one's life when one is seeking the larger and more complex skills of intuition and knowing.

Make a list of things that you can do to ground yourself in daily life.

1._____

2._____

3._____

4._____

5._____

6._____

How might you bring spirituality and compassion, insight and wisdom to each action and maintain that grounded connection?
_____
_____
_____
_____
_____

LISTENING TO THE QUIET INNER VOICE
This can be called the "oou" factor. "OOU" you might see something you do not like. "OOU" you might see something you do like! Astounding as it seems many people ignore or actively dismiss as wrong the promptings of their inner voice

on matters of importance. Often the inner voice provides a warning or information which is not welcome.

Make a choice to actively listen to the inner voice for a week. Write down each time the information comes through.

1._____

2._____

3._____

4._____

5._____

6._____

ALLOWING YOURSELF TO ACT ON WHAT YOU HEAR WHEN THE INTERNAL VOICE IS QUIET

You have noticed information coming through. Now what? In many individuals just recognizing that information is available is the most difficult part. Many of us have dismissed the information we are receiving as fast as it is comes to us. So allowing the information to come to consciousness, even when it is uncomfortable is an important first step. Remember, if the information is contrary to what you want to take place, denial of the information is a sure way to make it happen. Instead, recognize that the information you have just received is situational. It is the best information you have at that moment. BUT the causes are not all made! Since the information has come in advance of the situation, the situation can be changed! So instead of following the pattern in our society of denial of truth, look at what is the truth at that moment, decide if that is what you want to make manifest or if you want to make a change. Then let the situation unfold or make changes as necessary.

Share three experiences where you allow yourself to act on your inner voice.

1._____
_____
2._____
_____
3._____
_____

NOTICING YOUR DISREGARD

One of the most difficult aspects of learning to pay attention to your intuition and flashes of insight is to learn to pay attention on the occasions when you would automatically dismiss the information without any exploration or focus. It is hard to interrupt that habit pattern. And in most people it is a habit pattern. And if you wish to follow this path this habit pattern needs to be interrupted so that you at least stop for a moment and recognize that some information has been made present.

Consider spending several days focusing on when information comes through as the natural process of a day. Write that information down.
1._____

2._____

3._____

Then pick one of the times that information generally comes through and pay direct attention to when and under what circumstances, you simply ignore the information. Write down on the same page under that time period, the type of information which came through. Write down if that information was useful. Make note of how many times in that period information is made available to you. List the type of information and the frequency of that type of information in that time period. Then select another time period and repeat this process.

Time * Type of information * Useful? * How often got info

_____
_____
_____
_____
_____
_____
_____
_____
_____
_____
_____
_____

NOTICING NOT WANTING TO HEAR

Once you notice the type of information you most often ignore, do some thinking about situations in the past that might have caused you to make that choice. Ask yourself, "is it still the right choice for me to ignore this type of information?" If it is then continue to ignore the information. If it has a use in your life consider spending one day a week in that time period or activity paying specific attention to the information which comes through. Write the information down. Intuitive information can be easy to forget in a life that is busy.

Try to follow through the change in focus for at least three months. It often can take that long a period of time to make a behavioral change and make it successfully.

A number of individuals who have tried this process have found that they were ignoring information which was related to a painful life episode or to situations which they felt they could not change. With a painful life episode you might consider following this process:

STEP 1: How would you have handled the situation differently given the information which you have today?

STEP 2: Determine how you might forgive yourself for making the choice you made.

STEP 3: Determine if there are any resources you need to establish so that if the situation happens again you can make a different and possibly more successful choice.

STEP 4: Put those resources in place.

STEP 5: Commit an act of forgiveness toward self. For example: buy flowers for your self. Go on a enjoyable hike. Meditate on a sunrise.

STEP 6: Appreciate that you are able to make a new choice.

HEALING THROUGH INTUITION WITH WISDOM

Another option is to use your developing intuitive skills to create healing for yourself. You might want to create a ceremony to celebrate a change in your focus and use some of your intuitive information to guide you while you develop the ceremony.

You might want to write in a journal the experience you have had in the recognition process and allow yourself to sit with a blank page and see if any related intuitive information becomes available.

Write it down and see how it relates to the issue you are addressing. Or you might want to commit an act of creation. Paint a painting, write a book, write a play, choreograph a dance, and in whatever medium you choose allow your developing intuitive skills to come out and play!

In whatever option you choose make a distinct behavioral change. And give yourself both the gift of sufficient time and plan the process of noticing so that you will be successful. For many people changing habit patterns is challenging. Remember to be as compassionate with yourself as you would be with others you might be helping.

FINAL EXERCISE CHAPTER 2. WORKBOOK:

Use this page to write down the key experiences that you have had as you learned in this chapter. Try to include things that you think will be among the most important stories to share with your future parishioner's/client's/student's.

_____
_____
_____
_____
_____
_____
_____
_____
_____
_____
_____
_____
_____
_____
_____
_____
_____

Workbook for Chapter Three

What is compassion?

Definition of compassion

Compassion is a form of sympathy. We will define compassion as being aware of, recognizing and wanting to help remedy the misfortunes of others through having deep sympathy, empathy, appropriate boundaries and the urge to take action.

Where does a spiritual connection fit?

True compassion comes from a combination of the recognition of something that needs repair, a spiritual connection, gratitude, and wisdom. Spiritual connection allows us to see the value which in woven into each and every beautiful work of art which is a person.

The calm spiritual connection can be created in a number of different ways.

1. Brain research has found a still point of thought that can be created through the process of doing neurofeedback. When this still point is achieved, in that moment an act of creation can be brought forth that allows for rightness to be re-established.

2. You may pray or meditate until a deep connection to the issue is established and path forward is seen.

3. You may simply see a need and a solution through a flash of insight.

4. You may recognize a need in the self to take action to create value in the world and seek an opportunity to take that action.

Describe an experience where you expressed compassion to another person.
What was the support which they needed?
How did you choose to support them?
What kinds of boundaries did you hold with the person?
What was your personal emotional response to your action of compassion?
What was the persons response to your compassionate act?

_____
_____
_____
_____
_____
_____
_____
_____
_____
_____
_____
_____

HOW TO DO FORGIVENESS OF SELF

Often within the act of redemption is the act of forgiveness. Allowing yourself to see the information which you have denied even to yourself in the past, and being willing to share this information as accurately as possible in an effort to aid another is a powerful and positive action. Guilt over the times you have not listened to the self, denied information, or have worked against the self is not unusual. However, guilt is a useless emotion unless we use it to move ourselves forward into a better perception of ourselves and others by taking actions to resolve the guilt.

To resolve the guilt one must forgive oneself. The following steps are one way to take that action:

1. Look at the situations in which mistakes or poor choices were made.
2. Notice the choice points and the situation from which the issue arose.

3. Now look carefully at the choices and decide what you might do differently when faced with a similar situation.

4. How might that choice have effected the original situations outcome?

5. Spend a few minutes giving yourself permission to act in this new way if a similar situation ever shows up again.

6. Now judge the forgive-ability given that you have created new options for behavior, you have recognized the error(s) made, and you have given yourself the option to do something new.

7. Then allow yourself to stand in the connection you have established to the Divine and let the forgiveness from that source flow through you.

8. Offer appreciation to yourself and appreciation to all that is for the change you have just made.

Practice forgiving yourself. List three separate issues around which you have difficulty or judgment. Go through the steps. Write in detail your experience of forgiving yourself around at least one of those issues.
What did you discover?
What was the easiest step in the process?
What was the most difficult step in the process?
How would you handle the situation if you were to experience it today?

What would the new outcome be?
_____
_____
_____
_____
_____
_____
_____
_____
_____
_____
_____
_____
_____
_____

How to Forgive the Other

Since life experience rarely happens in a void, it is not unusual to have to forgive others as well as ourselves. When you are sharing intuitive information, it may be resisted or denied. You may be criticized for the information which you have shared. You may be criticized for the form in which you shared the information, not immediately giving the person who is receiving the information exactly what they want. Strive to come to the process of the persons challenging response from the place of calm-passion.

If you have shared the intuitive information from a place of truth and wisdom, then begin with a recognition that humans have a great deal of resistance to change.

This resistance to change can take many forms:

- It can arise from the level of electrical resistance produced across physical tissue related to nervous system response.
- The emotional, mental, and/or spiritual responses to the change when a highly charged issue arises.
- Memories of similar life situations.
- Or the naming of a truth which can be a relief and/or an immediate burden.

To that end, the ability to forgive the person receiving the information when they respond aggressively to intuitive information which we have shared from a place of truth is important.

A similar process to the forgiveness of self can be used to forgive another with the key difference that first you must recognize that you are not responsible for another persons reactions.

Practice forgiving another person. List three separate issues around which you have difficulty or judgment with another person. Go through the steps.
Write in detail your experience of forgiving one of them around at least one of the issues.
What did you discover?
What was the easiest step in the process?
What was the most difficult step in the process?
How would you handle the situation if you were to experience it today?
What would the new outcome be?
_____
_____

Workbook for Chapter Four

Basic Methods of Accessing Intuitive Information?

While this book describes a set of steps which can be used to develop your intuitive skills there is no substitution for practice. These are skills, similar to learning to type or drive a car or parachuting. You must put in just as much time to learn these skills as you did learning to type or drive a car or jump out of a perfectly good airplane. There is no substitution for skills drill. There is no substitution for practicing methods to speak with people. There is no substitution for drilling until you have reliable accuracy in the information you receive and share. Please do each of these drills until you feel competent in the process of recognizing how you receive information and what kinds of information you are good at receiving.

Reaching up
Ground, center and align with the Divine. Then take a series of three deep breaths. One to relax, one to experience and one to focus. Then feel for the center point at the top of your head from inside your head. Once you establish the connection to the center point at the top of your head, then, using your creative mental aspect, see a line 90 degrees to the

top of your head. Slide your consciousness up that line until you feel a small amount of pressure and perhaps hear a quiet pop sound. Then sink into contact with that point and reach for your connection to the Divine. Sink into contact with the Divine in whatever form is correct for your beingness and allow yourself joy and gratitude in the contact.

Do this practice three times and write down your experience of the process. How was each experience the same? How was each experience different?

1._____

2._____

3._____

ALLOWING RETURN FLOW OF INFORMATION

Once the connection is established it is important to actually allow the flow of information to come back into your consciousness. This is a surrender/allowing space. One surrenders to the will of the Divine and allows the information to slide back along the pathway you personally have established (so that you know the information is clean and safe to receive). Then you breathe and sit in allowing. See what information comes to consciousness.

Practice once a day for six weeks and ask yourself a question to which you really want an answer. With practice once a day each day for about 6 weeks most individuals can establish a connection which allows them to get and share information in a real time session with a client or parishioner. Remember the imagery will come in your personal unconscious/body vocabulary. Be careful not to interpret. State the images clearly and with precision.

List at least one question each week that you have asked and the answer that you received.

1._____

2._____

3._____

4._____

5._____

6._____

ALIGNING WITH THE LIGHT OF TRUTH

Aligning with the light of truth should be practiced for several weeks as a separate process before being used for an intuitive read. To align with the light of truth one begins with the breath. Take at least three breaths to clear your mind and begin to focus. Then using thought as a tool to direct the energy and focus make the connection to the Divine in whatever form is correct for you. Deepen your ground once the connection to the Divine is established. Then think about facts which are true about you. Things that are simple. For example: your street address, your mothers name, your name, how old you are... Think about 20 facts and with each one send a pulse of energy using the breath and focus up to the Divine. Then feel and watch the flow of energy that comes back down to you along the same pathway. In a short period of time the flow of energy which comes back down will glow with the light of truth of the information which you have been sending up. Then sit in that flow of light and simply breathe and feel. How does that light feel on your skin? How does that light feel as it washes through your body and into the ground? In this process you are literally a link between the Divine and earth and aligning/sitting in truth as a practice place is very important for your ability to recognize the sensate experience of truth verses any other type of current flow.

Practice moving in and out of truth so that you can clearly feel when you are correctly aligned. This is a skill. You must drill this skill until you can link to the light of truth easily and comfortably. It generally takes several weeks of 10 min a day practice to establish a firm link. Give yourself the grace of time and do the skills drill. You will work better without feeling guilty because you cannot establish a connection. Instead move from a place of compassion and accuracy.

Practice this each day for six days. How does it feel to establish the connection? How does it feel to be in the connection? How does it feel to disconnect?

1._____
_____
2._____
_____
3._____

4._____

5._____

6._____

REACHING INTO THE HEART

The method of "reaching into the heart" is a way that a kinesthetic may improve their accuracy and share what is truthful keeping to the actual limits of the information which they receive. It is a three step method. Again, one begins by grounding, centering and aligning. Next, one specifically aligns with the light of truth. Finally, one sinks into the center of the tips of the heart chakra. Wait in that connection until the images and colors which are being perceived become still.

Then you ask the question the person is seeking information about as precisely as possible of your own heart. See what kind of information you receive as a result. Only share the actual information which you perceive. Share no interpretations. Share no extra information and be sure that you are sitting in the light of truth in all of your sharing.

Even if you are not primarily kinesthetic this is a good skill to learn. Practice on six friends. List the question and any information your receive.

1._____

2._____

3._____

4._____

5._____

6._____

SEARCHING THE WATERS OF THE BODY

If you are a visual you can also search the waters of the body which store memory to gain information. Ask for permission before using this form of information access as doing a read on an individual without their permission can be perceived by that individual as a violation of their space. Once you have permission, you will once again begin with ground, center and align your heart. Then define the question which the parishioner/client wants answered as precisely as possible.

Charge the question and send it and a single pulse to the person's field. See what lights up. Then charge the individual areas which light up and watch the "movies" of the person's life experience which will display in the field. Watch each area from dullest (longest in the field and least charged) to brightest. Then spend several minutes thinking through what you have seen and combining the information into a cohesive whole. Remember this is just more information.

Practice this six times. Write down the question, what you saw as you pulsed the field and what you see as a response in the person's field.

1._____
_____
_____
_____

2._____
_____
_____

3._____
_____
_____

4._____
_____
_____

5._____
_____
_____

6._____
_____
_____

SURRENDERING TO THE DIVINE

Once your connection is established there will be times when information will simply come to you. It is often unexpected and not information you necessarily want to have. Be patient with yourself in those instances. There will generally be a good reason for why you will have received the information.

If you are patient, the reason will come to light and you will be happy to have the information.

At the same time, if you are receiving information out of context in quantities which are debilitating you have the right and obligation to say "stop." Send the stop up your established connection to the light of truth and until you say yes to receiving information again the flow will generally stop. If it does not check and see if you are properly disconnecting at the end of a session. You do not want to leave the connection in place 24-7. You want to connect, get the necessary information and disconnect. We live in a sea of energy and to maintain connection to this level of flow becomes overwhelming.

As you practice over the next 6-12 weeks list any time you get continuing information. What was the type of information? Was it useful? Was there a specific time of day or physical environment where you received this information? How did you finally disconnect?

1._____

2._____

3._____

4._____

5._____

6._____

Practice connecting and disconnecting. To properly disconnect, ground, center, align and pull all extended currents back into the self. Then take three cleansing breaths and deliberately change your minds focus to something mundane like doing laundry or car pools or getting out a newsletter.

How did it feel to connect and what was your experience of disconnecting?

1._____

2._____

3._____

4._____

5._____

6._____

ROLLING FORWARD OR BACKWARD IN TIME

Another method of accessing information useful to your parishioner/client is to move forward or backward in time. This takes specific training in forward projection or regression. It is not to be done lightly and not to be done without correct training as it often uncovers significant issues. It should only be done when the parishioner/client has the correct psychological support system.

While it can provide useful information, anything involving memory is suspect and can be manipulated. Generally, it is wise to send the parishioner/client for help in this area with someone who is correctly trained to do this type of work. Referral to a trained therapist or hypnotherapist is usually a good choice if progression or regression work is necessary to support a parishioner/client properly.

We will do these exercises in class so that everyone is supervised during the process. If you are not a class member and wish to learn this skill please feel free to contact me.

Connecting to core

One of the methods of accessing information and for moving a parishioner/client into a deeper connection with themselves is to "access core." This is an esoteric technique which has been around for about 6000 years. To begin this process start with grounding, centering and aligning. Then breathe into the belly. Shift your consciousness into the center of the center of the belly and breath. Begin to watch with the mind's eye and look for a spark to flash in the center of the center of the belly (lower tien tien). When you "see" the spark breath into the spark. You are essentially adding oxygen to the flame. Breathing into the spark, grow it until the charged area fills the belly. Then acting as a tuning fork, brush the edges of your field on the outside edges of the parishioners/clients field. Allow the resonating pattern of the charged field of your core, to vibrate across the field connections and watch as the core in the parishioner/client lifts to match. Coach the individual as they too breathe into this connection. They will be making a connection to the core of themselves and will have an opportunity to perceive how beautiful they are. From this place of connection, they can ask questions of themselves and seek answers internally.

Often in this process you will have to hold their core lifted with your own core lift. This is very important as it can be hard to see your beauty when you are also looking at perceived wrongness. Maintain your core lift with breath. **There is no actual physical contact with the parishioner/client at any time in the process.**

Practice in lifting your core can be done over a period of a week or so. Once you have identified how to access your core, lift your core. Practice it six times and share what you felt (both your physical sensate reaction and your emotional response) each time.

1._____

2._____

3._____

4._____

5._____

6._____

Then practice lifting your core to lift another person's core. Remain with your core lifted for a period of time (not longer than 3 min to start), supporting the other persons connection.

What is your experience of this process?

Did you see the beauty of the self and the beauty in the other person?

Practice it six times with friends and family and share your experience.

1._____

2._____

3._____

4._____

5._____

6._____

USING THE MINDS EYE ACCESS

One of the most common ways a natural connection is established to intuitive information is through access to the "minds eye." For this access you must have an awareness of how your brain feels, where you think from inside your head and perceive how information flows into your body and your brain.

Grounding, centering and aligning begins the process. Then three cleansing breaths to begin the process of internal focus. Feel where you think from as a perceptive process from inside the self.

Is it in the center of the head? If yes, describe the types of information you are receiving.

_____
_____
_____
_____
_____
_____
_____

Is it to one side of the head? If yes, describe the types of information you are receiving.

_____
_____
_____
_____
_____

How does it feel to think from the back of the head verses the front of the head? Do you get any information when you ask yourself a question? How do you perceive emotions when you think from the back of the head?

_____
_____
_____
_____
_____

How does it feel to think from the bottom of the head verses the top? Do you get any information when you ask yourself a question? How do you perceive emotions when you think from the bottom of the head?

_____
_____
_____
_____
_____

Once you have perceived the differences in how you think, based on where you think inside your own head, move the thought into the center of the head. Breathe and be. Now move to the observer self. Ask yourself a specific question and watch where the answer comes. As you watch what happens notice where the information enters/appears inside your head.

List the question and where the answer comes from inside your head. Do this at least three times.

1._____

_____

2._____

_____

3._____

_____

Think about an image which you have seen in a movie and watch where the image comes into your brain. Then allow a memory of something to come and notice how the images related to that memory enter the brain. Then remember something that had significant emotional impact and notice how the images enter the brain. List the type of image, the image itself and where it enters the brain for each of these processes. Do this practice at least three times.

1._____

_____

2._____

_____

3._____

_____

Final Exercise for Chapter 4. Workbook:

This is a skill. Spend 10 minutes each day for two weeks practicing connecting to this minds eye. Over the course of the two weeks make note of your questions, impressions, information and when you need to change where you perceive inside your head for that type of information input. This will help you develop a road map for your own future.

Workbook for Chapter Five

Interpretation of Information

Practice sharing information specifics. Be as accurate as possible. Do not embellish or interpret. And pay attention to how, what type and where you are accessing the information inside your own head. List exactly what you see. Nothing extra. Do this exercise at least three times.

_____
_____
_____
_____
_____
_____
_____
_____
_____
_____
_____
_____
_____
_____
_____
_____
_____
_____
_____
_____

THE EGO SELF AND THE NEEDS OF THE UNCONSCIOUS

You will also want to discover if and when the information you are getting is noise. Noise is not unusual when accessing intuitive information. Noise happens in several different ways:

1. As you start to access intuitive information if there is noise on the wave/signal that you are trying to access then you may get images that have nothing to do with the information you are trying to access. You can recognize this situation from a buzzing sound as you access the information, or a series of images that are random in nature and feel far removed from the information you are seeking, they will feel disconnected and distant or the images will make you feel as if you need to gag. In this situation say to yourself, "this is noise and it is not in truth." Then deliberately align yourself with the light of truth and flow light into the wave to clear the noise off of it.

2. Noise on the wave may happen when you deny correct information. Your unconscious will then try to send you signals that you have liked in the past to satisfy you. When you get a series of images that you have seen in the past that have been correct, go back to the image that you received first. Then breathe and allow that image to come back in. Do not interpret. Simply see what is there.

3. Noise may happen when you try to superimpose interpretations on the information as it is coming in. Be aware as you receive information you need to be

passive, receptive and deliberately stop the brain from deciding what the information means. Instead simply see what comes in.

Write down one experience when you determined noise was getting in the way of accurate information. Explore what kind of noise and why it might have happened.

_____
_____
_____
_____
_____
_____
_____
_____
_____
_____
_____
_____
_____

Are you aware as a practitioner of why you are engaging in this work?
What has brought you to this pathway?
Is it altruism or the need to control someone else?
Is it compassion for another or the need to acquire love for yourself?
Is it joy in the sharing or the need to be right?
Is it gratitude for the connection to all of the grace and majesty that is this amazing world we live in or the need to just feel a connection to someone, anyone?

Write two paragraphs and define the nature of your personal relationship to this work:

_____
_____
_____
_____
_____
_____
_____
_____
_____
_____
_____
_____
_____
_____
_____

What are five things you can do to nurture yourself outside of the parishioner/client contact in the ways that you need and that are satisfying?

1._____

2._____

3._____

4._____

5._____

WHAT IS YOUR UNCONSCIOUS VOCABULARY

Keep a log of meanings of images, tastes, smells, colors, sense of heat or cold etc. Over time you will see patterns in the type of image/taste/smell/sound which you can identify with greater specificity.

Image * Taste Smell * Color * Temp * Wet/Dry/Dusty
_____
_____
_____
_____
_____
_____
_____
_____
_____
_____
_____
_____
_____

What kind of information do you regularly deny as being accurate? When you make the list notice if it is one specific type of information that you regularly deny as being correct.
_____
_____
_____
_____
_____
_____
_____

ARE YOU STEREO-TYPING OR LOOKING AT CATEGORIES OF BEHAVIOR

Write down a time you made assumptions about a person you had just met. What might you do differently if you were meeting them now?

_____
_____
_____

ARE YOU SHARING PHONY PSYCHOBABBLE

What are the 6 types of information you are never allowed to share?

1. _____
2. _____
3. _____
4. _____
5. _____
6. _____

DON'T INTERPRET! SAY WHAT YOU SAW EXACTLY

What is the type of information that you have the most difficulty sharing? List three things you could do to share the information with greater accuracy.

1. _____
_____

2. _____
_____

3. _____
_____

Workbook for Chapter Six

Appropriate Sharing of Intuitive Information

Make note of the aspects below. Select something in your life and see if you can specify each of the aspects noted:

1. The appearance: the external and perceptible forms, or physical aspects of life.

2. The nature: the spiritual or mental aspects of life.

3. The entity: the form that manifests the appearance and nature.

4. The power: the inherent power or energy of life.

5. The influence: the action produced when latent energy is activated.

6. The internal cause: the cause latent in life which has a corresponding effect, which can remain dormant.

7. The relation: the external cause which activates the internal cause.

8. The latent effect: the effect produced in the depths of life when an internal cause is triggered by an external cause.

9. The manifest effect: what actually happens that you can perceive.

10. The consistency from beginning to end: the perfect integration of these factors into every moment of life.

_____
_____
_____
_____
_____
_____
_____
_____
_____
_____
_____
_____

What are three important things to keep in mind when dealing with individuals from other cultures?

1._____

2._____

_____

3._____
_____

WHAT TO DO WHEN YOU GET NOTHING

Write down an experience of when you were practicing and got nothing in the way of information.
What mistakes did you make?
What did you do correctly?
Why might getting nothing in terms of information be good and why might it be difficult?
How did you handle this at the time?

Be as detailed as possible so that you can use this information as a reference in the future.

Support system assessment

Before you share information of any kind with a parishioner/client it is important to assess their support system.

You might ask several of the following questions:

1. Are there family members or close friends available for support?

2. If there are family members available, is it a functional family. Do those members in fact have the capacity to support?

3. Does this person have an appropriate outside support system? (Be sure to have a referral list available for your local area.)

4. Does the person have appropriate financial means to get the support they need?

5. Does the person have the appropriate physical means to get the support that they need?

6. What part of these things need to be in place prior to your sharing your intuitive information?

7. How will you support the parishioner/client in getting the support they need? (This should be done with appropriate boundaries.)

8. Once this support system is in place, when will you share your intuitive information.

If the support system is in place then sharing you information in an appropriate manner is not an issue. But it is your responsibility to be sure the person has a support system in place prior to sharing any information which will be challenging for them to hear.

Do a support system assessment on three different people. Where did each one have support and what areas if any were they lacking in support?

1._____
_____
2._____
_____
3._____
_____

POWER AND CONTROL

Take a careful look at the list below. Then write three short paragraphs on how you personally hold power and what you try to control in your life. Then spend a few minutes thinking about what you might like to change about that process. List what changes you would like to make.

1. If I make myself appear powerful the person will do what I tell them and then their life will get better because of what I told them to do.

2. If I make myself appear powerful then the person will back off, go away and stop questioning me.

3. If I make myself appear powerful lots of people will come and ask me for advice and this will mean I am a good person.

4. If I make myself appear powerful then I will keep myself safe.

5. If I make myself appear powerful then people will love me so then I can love myself.

6. In what situations do you feel uncertain? Why do you experience that uncertainty? Is that uncertainty appropriate?

7. When you share information with a parishioner/client what do you gain in power? What do you loose in power?

8. What does the parishioner/client gain in power? What does the parishioner/client lose in power?

_____
_____
_____
_____
_____
_____
_____
_____

LIMITS OF THE INTUITIVE

While intuitive information may be tremendously valuable to the parishioner/client each person has their own sense of timing on which to act on information. Each person will have their own interpretation of the information which you share. Each person will have their own choices to make based on the information you share.

What are the three key aspects that are limits to the way in which you share intuitive information?

1._____

2._____

3._____

What are the three things you will make sure of about the information prior to sharing?

1._____

2._____

3._____

What do you need to watch for in the parishioner's/client's behavior as you are sharing? And how will you handle it when you see the particular behavior?

1._____

2._____

3._____

Workbook for Chapter Seven

Inside and Outside the self

The skills building which allows for the development of appropriate boundaries, accurate intuitive information and the separation of emotional noise is not simple. It takes time. It takes drill. It takes discipline.

You are working with another being and that act is sacred. You have a deep responsibility to support that individual to the best of your ability. So do not fail yourself. Do the drill. Develop solid skills.

What are three important boundaries to hold as you work with people?

1._____
_____

2._____
_____

3._____
_____

Gained and lost opportunities

Have a discussion with a person whom you know.
What do they think of change?
When do they think change is positive?
What are some of the ways that they think change can be made in a way that is more fluid?

_____
_____
_____
_____

Fear as a choice

Write down an experience of a time you chose to fear.
With your new knowledge how might you have handled the situation differently?
What might you if you encounter a similar situation in the future?

_____
_____
_____
_____

Fear of Being Noticed

Write down an experience of a time you were afraid of being seen for the amazing being that you are.
With your new knowledge how might you have handled the situation differently?
What might you if you encounter a similar situation in the future?

_____
_____
_____
_____

TECHNIQUES OF DOWN REGULATION AND FORGIVENESS

What is one experience that you have had that you regret? What steps will you take to forgive yourself? List you plan and then take action. When you have forgiven yourself, write down how you feel about the process.

_____
_____
_____
_____
_____
_____

CHOOSING JOY AND HAPPINESS

What is one thing that you can do each day for yourself to create joy in your life?

_____
_____
_____
_____

What is one thing that you can do for someone else to support their creating joy in their life?

_____
_____
_____
_____

Final Exercise Chapter 7. Workbook:

Use this page to write down how you are both different and how you are the same as each and every person with whom you cross paths. Spend some time and see if you can share points that you have found that unify humanity on fundamental levels. Then describe how you will find and discover value in each and every person you meet in the future.

Workbook for Chapter Eight

Final Words

Final Exercise Chapter 8. workbook:
Use this page to write down what are the most important things which you will need to remember as you move forward into the future. What insights have you had that are important? Write down a list to help you remember that which you might forget so that twenty years from now you will read it and understand it to a new level.

_____
_____
_____
_____
_____
_____
_____
_____
_____
_____
_____
_____
_____
_____
_____

Workbook Appendix A.

Ethics of Sharing

The ethical sharing of information with clients and parishioners is critical. Not all people will have the support systems necessary to be able to hear and receive the information a practitioner receives. In addition, not all people will have a personal paradigm that makes them comfortable receiving this type of information. Always be careful and respectful of the person in your sharing. Sharing information in a way that creates a power dynamic with the person is to be avoided. Remember that no medical or psychological diagnosis may be made at any time unless the practitioner has that training and skill within their legally defined scope of practice.

Steps to take to assess if the information is correct and to be shared:

1. Is it true? If you are not sure then work from the position that it is not true and do not share the information until you are sure.

2. Have you verified it with more than one sense? Be sure that you can verify the information with more than one sense.

3. Can another person verify your impressions? Get another opinion especially if you may not be clean in this area.

4. Is it kind? If it is not do not tell them.

5. Does the person need to know the information? If they do not need to know this information do not share it. If they do need to know the information share it with discernment.

6. What will you gain by sharing the information? Be very clear. You owe it to yourself not to create negative karma.

7. What will the person gain by receiving the information? Run possibilities in your head. Expect the unexpected.

8. Can you gift the information to the person in such a way that you say the words without blame and judgment? If you cannot then do not say it until you can. Do your processing at home not in the session. The parishioner/client is not your therapist.

9. Are you making a medical diagnosis? If so is it within your scope of practice?

10. Does the person have adequate support for the period that they are processing the information that you have provided to them?

11. If they do not see that they get support before you share this information with them.

Workbook Appendix B.

Practice Sharing Information Exercises

1. Find the body centric language and explain how it relates to the situation.

2. What is the persons primary defense? This exercise is based on a ten layer defense model. For more information: Connor. M., *"Advanced Body Reading."*

Example A: "I keep telling him the way I do it is right! And he does not pay any attention to what I am saying. Nor does he do things the way I am telling him."

Example B: "You really want me to do that? Why would you want me to do that? I shouldn't have to do that…"

Example C: "You will do what I tell you. Go."

3. How will you ask the following question? What should the focus be of this session?

4. You have just seen something which may be difficult for the person to hear about. What will you say to them? How much will you say? And why might you limit the information which you are sharing?

5. Is there transference from the client on to the practitioner? (positive / negative) How will you handle that transference? What kind and how will you set the appropriate boundaries?

6. Is there transference from the practitioner on to the client? (positive / negative) How will you handle that transference? What kind and how will you set the appropriate boundaries?

7. What types of questions would be good to use in a session where the client makes the following statements?

Example A: "I really do not know why I came. My wife made the appointment."

Example B: "I just do not feel like I am making any progress with my life. I'm stuck."

Example C: "I am just so tired."

ABOUT THE AUTHOR

MELINDA H. CONNOR

Beginning her training as a child in the energy skills, she is the founder of Earthsongs Holistic Consulting & Executive Director of the International Journal of Healing & Caring. She is the lineage holder for the Resonance Modulation energy skills training program. Between Harvard, Wellesley, University of San Francisco, California Coast University, University of Arizona, American Military University and seminary programs, she holds three master's degrees and two doctorates.

Dr. Connor was trained in research as an NIH T-32 postdoctoral fellow in the Program in Integrative Medicine from the University of Arizona. Professor Connor, is the former chair of the board of directors for the National Alliance of Energy Practitioners and is also both nationally certified by NCCOEP and board certified by the American Alternative Medicine Association.

She is a lifetime fellow of the Royal Society of Medicine in the UK, professor emerita and former research director at Akamai University, and the author of ten books. Professor Connor has received both international awards from *CEO Today Magazine* and *Finance Monthly* and US recognition from the *California State Legislative Assembly*. Named a top research scientist by the World Qigong Congress and Marquis Who's

Who, she was recently bestowed with the prestigious title of Empowered Woman of the Year for 2024 by the International Association of Top Professionals (IAOTP). This recognition is a testament to her outstanding leadership, unwavering dedication, and unparalleled commitment to the industry.

WWW.DRMELINDAHCONNOR.COM
WWW.EARTHSONGS.COM
WWW.IJHC.ORG

www.ingramcontent.com/pod-product-compliance
Lightning Source LLC
Chambersburg PA
CBHW051100230426
43667CB00013B/2379